monsoonbooks

INVISIBLE TRADE II

Gerrie Lim is the bestselling author of *Invisible Trade: High-Class Sex for Sale in Singapore*, his exposé of the escort business in Southeast Asia, and *In Lust We Trust: Adventures in Adult Cinema*, his memoir of a decade spent covering the erotica industry in Los Angeles, California, where he previously lived for fifteen years as a freelance writer contributing to *Billboard*, *Details*, *LA Style*, *LA Weekly*, *Penthouse*, *Playboy* and *The Wall Street Journal*. This is his fifth book.

ALSO BY GERRIE LIM

* *Invisible Trade:*
High-class sex for sale in Singapore

* *In Lust We Trust:*
Adventures in Adult Cinema

Inside the Outsider:
A Decade of Shooting the Pop Culture Breeze

Idol to Icon:
The Creation of Celebrity Brands

* *(published by Monsoon Books)*

INVISIBLE TRADE II

Secret lives and sexual intrigue in Singapore

GERRIE LIM

monsoon

monsoonbooks

Published in 2008
by Monsoon Books Pte Ltd
52 Telok Blangah Road
#03-05 Telok Blangah House
Singapore 098829
www.monsoonbooks.com.sg

ISBN: 978-981-05-9209-7

"Breakfast With Tiffany" cover photograph©Milos Sadik
Author photograph©Michael Goh

National Library Board Singapore Cataloguing in Publication Data
Lim, Gerrie.
Invisible trade II / Gerrie Lim. – Singapore : Monsoon Books, 2008.
p. cm.
ISBN-13 : 978-981-05-9209-7 (pbk.)
1. Sex-oriented businesses – Singapore. 2. Prostitution – Singapore. 3.
Prostitutes – Singapore. I. Title.
HQ243.A5
306.74095957 -- dc22   OCN221155999

Printed in Singapore

12 11 10 09 08   1 2 3 4 5 6 7 8 9

Once again, for P.H.

"Love you long time!"

Contents

Preface

Free from desire, you realize the mystery
Caught in desire, you only see the manifestations.

—Lao Tsu

Back in October 2006, on board Singapore Airlines flight SQ2 bound for San Francisco, I read Kate Holden's astonishing memoir, *In My Skin*, about her life as a heroin-addicted prostitute in her hometown of Melbourne, Australia.

She had begun by hailing cars on the streets of St Kilda and then graduated to more upscale escorting before deciding that her smack habit was detrimental to, well, pretty much everything. With her personal survival at stake, she cleaned up and finally wrote her amazing book, in the process winning the Judy Duffy Award for literary excellence. One particular passage summed up my own thoughts as I was preparing to write this one, the much-requested sequel to *Invisible Trade: High-Class Sex for Sale in Singapore*, published in 2004.

My intention was to uncover aspects of the sex industry not previously dealt with in that book and her words excited me, rather appropriately, like a drug rush.

At times I was disconcerted by the aggression of sex: a friendly man's face distorted by the ferocity of pleasure; the greedy ruthlessness of sexual momentum. It could still frighten me, beneath everything. People became strangers, and I could do nothing but cling to arms and ribs and hips as the face above me darkened with blood and I understood that I could only rush up to meet this force, or be battered by it. It was easier to mock the fervor of lust than to admit its fearful power. And I reminded myself that I was the one sought; it was I who was in control. These men, I thought, were diminished by their need.

There were men who cloaked their nervousness in disdain, and men who hid their disdain with charm. I enjoyed the game of guessing what each man would be like, and being confounded so often . . . "You're too good to be here," they still murmured to me. Just as they had in the cars of St Kilda.

"So are you," I'd say, but I'd take their hands and kiss their mouths to make sure they'd keep coming back.

Here then, in the pages that follow, are more true stories coated with eerily similar disdain and charm. I sought to unravel and demystify two key areas: the secretive "double lives" led by these girls and the reasons why some men habitually need to spend money for sex. Both involve addiction to a degree, and both are fed by deep existential forces fraught with anger and pain, often disguised as carnal longing.

There's the girl who works at a public relations agency by day and moonlights as an escort by night, with neither her office colleagues nor her parents nor (even more amazingly) her boyfriend knowing. There's the girl who married her much older client, a wealthy Caucasian expatriate who spends little time in Singapore, a perfect situation that enabled her to continue escorting without his knowledge (well, perfect that is, until he found out). There's the *karaoke*-bar *mamasan* who deals in wild and wanton girls from mainland China, and the American male escort who gets paid by visiting Shanghai socialites for his companionship both in and out of their hotel bedrooms.

There's the university student who freelances as a bondage model, paid to struggle and squirm while rope-tied as her client watches her and masturbates. Why do men pay for this? Ask the Australian gentleman with a penchant for Filipinas, who cruises the basement bars of a well-known Singapore hotel. And the Englishman who went on a self-professed "sex bender" in the Singapore red-light district of Geylang following his own divorce. And the self-proclaimed diehard sex tourist from Los Angeles who came to Southeast Asia to sample its professional paragons of feminine perfection, finally facing his nemesis among the nightbirds of Singapore.

All this and more, folks, in the hope that these disparate views will help to enrich our collective understanding of an industry that remains, for good reason, the world's oldest and most mystifying.

As with the previous book, this is not a work of fiction, though names and nationalities (and, upon specific request, even locations) were changed in order to protect my interviewees' privacy. And, once again, nothing in this book is written to dissuade anyone, whether escort or client, from their chosen lifestyle.

Gerrie Lim
Singapore

PART ONE

Sirens with Secrets

An Almost Imaginary Life

She loves the sound of her chosen name, she says, and didn't know until much later that it means "illusion." But it's so very fitting, of course, since that's exactly her job description.

Maya laughs. She's proud to be a high priestess of illusion and even came up with a running joke in honor of her name: By day, she works in public relations but by night she works in, misspelling intended, pubic relations.

On one occasion, however, the joke was literally on her instead. "One guy wanted me to shave in front of him, to shave my pubic hair," she recalls, "and yes, I did it. Some guys like girls shaved and others don't like that, so I don't know, it's hard to accommodate everyone. Some like me bare, some like me with a lot of hair.

"Some hair down there looks more natural, doesn't it? I think so. Anyway, this guy wanted me bare and paid me an extra S$50. It was my first time actually doing that. I should have asked him for more!"

Pubic relations, what kind of work was that for a sweet girl like her? Well, she could quit her day job if she wanted to, from the rave reviews she's received from her customers, not to mention the somewhat disproportionate income gap that results from such adoration. Hot damn, surely she *must* be good! Why else would so many of these guys keep calling to book her again?

Moonlighting for Maya, it seems, has really become a way of life. At the escort agency where she works four nights a week, she brings in the most repeat business of any of the girls. Clients have whisked her away to New York and Hong Kong and several places in Australia, and she even enjoyed an island retreat off the coast of West Malaysia with a famous Hollywood movie star. She remembers digging her nails into his back, and wondering if those marks would ever show up on-screen.

Back in Singapore, she's her agency boss's numero uno go-to girl for the big overnight jobs, where she stays with a client in his hotel suite till the next morning. She has, at any given time, between twenty to thirty "regulars" and she estimates she's had sex with at least a hundred guys. The exact number eludes her since she doesn't keep track anymore, because she's lost count. Just like the number of taxis ferrying her across Singapore, and the many hotel suites she's slept in.

"Well, being an escort is about pleasing people, so it is a form of public relations," she quips. Her daylight hours are spent at a small firm specializing in banking and technology. "My title is public relations consultant. I do research for presentations and I'm still a junior executive so I'm still learning. I started out as a part-time receptionist, as an intern while I was still in school, and then got a full-time job after I finished my diploma in mass communications."

The job, she knows, affords the perfect cover for her. "Naturally, I'm a friendly person, but my escort job has taught me to go one step higher. And when I'm not working, I do see my friends and some of them now ask me, 'What do you do? What are you working as?' I tell them I work in P.R. I'm on *Friendster* and I have my pictures on there and I go overseas all the time so when they check the site, they notice that I go overseas a lot and that's why they ask me what I do. A lot of these people are very *kaypoh*—such busybodies! I tell them I have to go overseas for travel, for my public relations work. Even my mother was asking me about it. But she doesn't anymore, not since I moved out of the house to live with my boyfriend."

Her boyfriend?!! Talk about leading a double life.

Indeed, while everyone knows about her respectable day job, nobody knows what she does after she leaves the office. Not her office colleagues, not her parents and definitely not her boyfriend. She even started escorting two months *after* she started dating him, and she gets away with it simply because they don't actually live together—he sleeps over at her condo only two or three nights a week and that's exactly how she likes it. Any more would seriously cramp her lifestyle.

And all this deft, illusory sleight-of-time is enhanced by the fact that she is a young Singaporean Muslim woman who actually grew up in Geylang Serai. Her father is of Indonesian descent, his ancestors hailing from Bandung, a town southeast of Jakarta, and her mother is pure Singapore Malay. The paradox is not at all lost on her.

"Of course, they don't know," she whispers, looking down, almost ashamed. "What would they say if they ever found out? Oh, they wouldn't say anything. They'd kill me. That's all, they'd just kill me!"

And so she must ensure that nobody *ever* finds out. Her cellphone is on silent mode most of the time and she's constantly checking to see who's calling. She admits to hitting a low point at the end of 2007. The day job was starting to bore her and she knew she would have to find something else to do, to prepare for the day when she will eventually leave the escort line. It's not enough to work hard, as they say, you have to work smart. At age twenty-four, she's still blessed with striking good looks—lustrous dark brown hair, a caramel complexion and a face that by itself could (and did) launch a hundred erections—and she was proud of her assets. But nobody, in truth, would want an escort over thirty. Those women either become *mamasan*s at KTV bars or run escort agencies themselves. Most of them leave the business altogether.

Maya says she would wake up sometimes feeling . . . well, she wasn't sure what it was. Empty? Lonely? She can't find the right word. So she applied for a new job, in a different line of work, to try escaping her sudden blue funk.

She didn't get past the first interview.

"I was the only shortlisted candidate but I turned down the offer," she recalls. "The pay was peanuts and the role was a huge step-down from what I've been doing." She sighs. She'd just received a call to go back to London, to meet with one of her regular clients there. All expenses paid including the flight and the hotel, and she would make several times what she was already making at the public relations firm, so how was it ever possible to leave?

"Aside from the money, I get sex," she says, "and I do have nice clients who buy me gifts and they have really helped me, they have helped me to work on my self-confidence. Slowly, they have actually helped me to build up my self-esteem."

She is no longer the deeply shy Malay girl she once was, but now that she's achieved what she set out to do, she can't seem to shake off whatever it was that first propelled her. It is almost as if she is hooked on a drug of some sort, like she needs the adrenaline—the high she gets from all the mystery and all the secrecy of her glamorous double life. The biggest rush, she admits, stems from the obvious fact that, clearly, she hasn't yet been caught. She is playing a cloak-and-dagger game, with an imaginable adversary, in an almost imaginary life.

"I like the risk involved," she says, nodding affirmatively and resolutely. "If you ask me what is my biggest risk in life, I would say this is the biggest risk, my being a working girl. I know what men like and I know what I provide. I'm a C-cup, I'm a 34-C, and I'm 157 meters tall, which is about five foot three, and I guess I'm what men all want. I did think about breast enlargement at one point but I got feedback from some of my clients, and they *all* said it was better that I stay natural. They all said I look perfect."

That, and perhaps also her being a third-generation Singaporean Muslim, which might be a turn-on for some of them? "Maybe so," she shrugs. "I don't know." A few of them, she discloses, have taken her out on the town purely for her company, to be seen at receptions and dinners with her. She doesn't mind serving as an adornment, since she gets at least S$300 for those gigs, where she merely has to look companionable, with no sexual acts solicited. "Sometimes, I'll twist them for more, especially if they are bankers or work for big companies!" she squeals. "I can see from where they live, where they stay, and all that. Often, the amount of my tip depends on their background and, from that, I can tell whether they're a good catch or not.

"And we *have* to catch them—I mean, really, that's what we do! And they all tip well. I make sure of that!"

Perhaps she has gotten way too good at it now. This wasn't where she thought she'd be back in April 2003, when she started out escorting while working as a receptionist. Pressed for cash, she decided to take the plunge by calling the escort agencies in the phone book.

"Yes, the *Yellow Pages*, I'm serious!" she says. There are, after all, eighteen pages of escort ads in the 2007/2008 Singapore *Yellow Pages*, starting with a lavish full-page color spread offering "discreet passion" and "fun-filled entertainment with our specially selected charming executive escorts." She liked the one that said it could provide "the ultimate feminine companionship" and was seeking girls looking for "a dynamic lifestyle and high income." That last part sold her on them, and she called.

"That's the agency where I work now," she reveals, "they interviewed me and I've been with them ever since. That was my first experience, as well—I had no connections back then, I had never even worked as a hostess or anything! But I do have a strong sex drive—I think on a scale of one to ten I would probably be an eight."

Only eight? How modest. "Well, I don't know, I mean, if I were to say ten, I would make myself out to be like a whore. That's why I say eight. People always have the wrong idea about us, anyway. They have this whole taboo idea, that we are to be seen as whores. Well, I think sometimes we may not be, and sometimes we can be. Escorting and prostitution, I would say they're almost alike. Except that in escorting we are more like companions. We offer companionship for the clients, while a prostitute just satisfies their sexual needs. Sometimes, these clients just want companionship, that's all."

Such was the case, in fact, with her very first client back in

2003—a wealthy American who was kind and compassionate and felt badly for her after learning it was her first-ever night on the job.

They spent three hours together, just talking. "It was my first time and I wasn't ready for it, and he was pretty okay with it," she remembers. "I actually didn't have sex at all with anyone for the first few times I went out on a job. I waited till I could see a better picture of it. There was fear, of course, definitely. The fear that something might go wrong, because he was a stranger, he was somebody I did not know. That, and the fear for my health. And then you have to have some kind of chemistry with the client. It all starts from there, naturally.

"After a few times, I decided to go for it. That was in 2003 and I can say now that the majority of clients I have been with are mostly respectable people. We have a clean image, actually, so I've never had problems with health or harassment. Not even once. The guys have all been respectful, even when they might have some fetishes, some fantasies."

Fantasies? "Yeah, you know, whatever I can do for them and all that," she says. "These guys all have different wants, different expectations, and we have to be there for them. You have to role-play and all that, and I do have clients who ask for those. Basically, you try to find guys who will treat you very well, you know, who will buy you dinner and have a good time with you. In the beginning, I tried to draw a boundary between my personal life and my client relationships, but after a while I took them like they were my friends and so you just go along with it."

Such humility, or was she understating the facts? Maya, as the escort grapevine has it, is "different" from the other girls because she apparently has ways to charm a man that most of them don't have. Mostly, she knows how to make them come back for more. She has the chops to hook a guy, by doing whatever it takes, and some of the other girls were apoplectic when they heard she is known to moan very, very loudly during sex—because this usually means you are exceptionally good at faking orgasms—and they'd also heard from clients that she was willing to give bareback blowjobs if the price was right. Sucking a stranger's cock *sans* condom, if he agrees to meet her "extra services" fee, might well seem gross to some of the other girls, but in truth it is serious professionalism at work. That is what a true sex worker does and Maya always delivers the goods. "With about seventy percent of my clients, I do it with a condom and the rest of them without, but only if they pay extra. Usually about S$200."

It also means you have to, almost literally, put up with shit. One of her clients got on top of her and, midway through his huffing and puffing, actually farted. "It was pretty smelly too," she laughs. "I was so embarrassed! I also had one Japanese guy who spanked me, very hard, and then he wanted me to swallow his saliva and swallow his cum. I got him to come in my mouth but I didn't swallow it. I don't like the taste! I usually let the guys ejaculate, like, around here." She mimics with her mouth closed, and points to her cheek and lower jaw. "That Japanese guy, though, also wanted me to drink his pee. I didn't, I refused to, that's really where I draw the line."

Yes, escorts, like anyone, have their own sexual parameters. "I've heard of a girl walking her client around on a leash, with a dog collar around his neck, weird stuff like that," Maya giggles. "I'm lucky to have gotten away with just spanking and sex!"

She almost didn't get away with guys falling in love with her—that single, inevitable occupational hazard that all escorts dread. "I've had that happen with three of my clients," she recalls. "One of them even asked me if I could move to be with him and wrote me love letters and all that. But he's married and I told him that it would be better if we stayed the way we are. Because he's married already, so this way he can keep his family and I can keep my job and we live our separate lives. And when he comes to Singapore, we can meet somewhere, which is what we do. I think a lot of married men use escorts, that's a fact. They want something different. It's not that they're bored in their marriage. They still love being married. But I think maybe they just want something different. If he's American and his wife is American, he tends to want me because he wants to try an Asian girl. Like we say in Malay, you cannot eat *nasi lemak* all the time, right?"

She laughs maniacally when told she is "exotic." That's happened one too many times, and she's over it. "Do I feel exotic?

Sometimes," she says. "Well, I have a job to do and I make sure I accomplish my mission—it's actually that simple. We are here to accomplish what we are here for. I'm very service-oriented and I make them feel like they're being entertained, as *much* as possible."

Perhaps it's easy enough to say that when the biggest perks of the job include a lot of travel, always at someone else's expense. In the past year, Maya has been to Hong Kong, Japan, Australia, Germany, and the United States. "I went to New York for a night job," she recalls. "A client booked me to go there. He paid for my flight and my hotel and I went there and he met me there, he picked me up."

She stayed at The Drake (now Swissotel The Drake, at 440 Park Avenue and East 56th Street) and calls it "the best experience of my life." The client was a rich Japanese businessman. "Not the spanking guy, another one. He had to meet a few of his other clients there so he needed me to accompany him. New York is really big. And you get to spend the entire day with the client. So I had to be with him 24/7, unless he had to go for a meeting. When that happens, he goes for his meeting and gives me shopping money, and I go out shopping. That's when you feel your secret life is worth it. Certainly in that case it was, because he paid me quite well.

"Australia was also interesting. I was there for a week, in Sydney and the Gold Coast. I traveled with the same guy, as his companion for both places, back and forth. It was my first time there and I quite liked it even though it was winter and quite cold. This was a couple of years back. My latest overseas trip was to Hong Kong, again in winter—just this past February. He's Australian, actually he's Australian Chinese, and he goes to Hong Kong on business. I stayed at the Marco Polo, in Kowloon. Unfortunately, I couldn't shop as much there. I wish I could have. The only shopping area was the one by the harbour. I didn't know where to go. Basically, we have to follow their arrangements. If they want us to stay with them the whole trip, then we have no choice. That time, he left me alone because he had his own room. It's actually quite unusual for me to have my own room on these trips. I prefer this kind of arrangement, though, because I have my own privacy."

The oddest consequence of her secret life, Maya says, was realizing how it was impacting her own personal relationship. Things with her boyfriend began to get strange, for reasons she hadn't expected. She began to demand more from him sexually, and also found herself needing more attention from him. "Because I give so much attention to my clients, so I need attention myself when I'm at home. You keep giving and giving and not receiving. I didn't expect him to buy me presents like my clients. What I really needed was nothing material, but rather attention and time."

They'd been together four years and were starting to hit a wall. "We're still working at it," she now reports, somewhat ruefully. "People think it's really weird that we're still together. You know, the fact is I was actually with him for two months when I started doing *this*, and he still doesn't know! That one amazes me, too."

One thing's for sure, though—he'll never understand how escort work has actually helped her with a lot of personal issues, including gaining self-confidence with her appearance.

"After you get by in this escort business, you learn how to personally groom yourself," she explains. "When I first started, I was all outrageous—even my bra was not matching!—and after a while, I learned to do some personal self-grooming on my hair, everything, top to toe. It's a must for a girl in this business to learn how to wear dresses well. Not that I was just wearing jeans at that time. When I started, I was wearing skirts and tops, but I was not really well groomed at that time. It's very important, actually, because it's the first impression that counts, the first thing the clients see." So when they all call back and she racks up the most repeat business at her agency, does she feel like she's become the equivalent of a rock star in her trade? "Yeah, I really do. It's an honor for me. But I try to keep a low profile. This business is very competitive. I am a bit modest. I don't want people to think I'm the greatest or I'm the best and then what if you don't meet their expectations? I like to be modest, and it's up to them to judge how I am. Whether I really am more special than the other girls, well, I don't know. Maybe that's a question the clients can answer. I have no idea."

She says that with the slightest hint of a smirk, like an imp up to some mischief again. "The issue of choice is important, I think. There's a difference between what I do and what the girls at Orchard Towers do, getting guys there to pay them S$250 for long-time. Most of the girls there could never be escorts, since they don't speak much English. I have a client who used to go there, he told me he gets tired of the same old conversations. You know, like, 'Oh, I like you, you so hansum man! I love you long time, love you only one!'

"But do I see myself as one step higher than these girls? Maybe. In a sense. Slightly. Does it make me feel proud of what I do? Again, yes. But slightly." She shrugs. That one's just so hard to explain. A whore anywhere is still a whore, but there are whores and there are whores. Just don't ever call her one. Because Maya is different, if only because she's been elevating her game to an art form, with social and sexual skills required of the sex industry's upper echelons. There are even historical precedents for this. Back in the days of ancient Greece, a woman's place was in the kitchen and at home, and the only women allowed to walk unaccompanied in public were actresses, musicians, and courtesans. The fact that she's a modern courtesan really does count for something, she says, and if some of the girls express envy at her jet-set lifestyle, well, that's their problem.

For there's a high price she pays to maintain the intricate web of secrecy that she has so elaborately spun. That's not something she expects anyone to understand. She looks pensive, and frowns a bit before speaking. "Back when I started, I remember being so nervous. For the first few bookings, to be honest, I was very nervous. I really was. *Very* nervous. I didn't know what to say and all that. But after a few drinks and so on, I overcame my nervousness. It took a while until I was comfortable and I got over the fear of doing this kind of thing. Now I have all kinds of clients and it doesn't bother me one bit. I've had sex with Caucasians, Indians, Malays, Indonesians, guys from all parts of the world. There's no better or worse—some are better, some are not. Some Indians are good and some white guys are not, and some white guys are good and some Indians are not. Some Koreans can be violent and the Japanese, too, they are very kinky and very rough. But I rarely get them because most Japanese clients prefer Chinese and Japanese girls.

"You meet people from all sorts of backgrounds and you share experiences. You have to be confident if you want to be in this line of work. Because if you go dining with them, you have to engage in intellectual conversations. I have encountered some boring clients, too, where most of the time I do all the talking. Most of these people are politicians. They tend to be very quiet. They don't talk a lot. They try to be discreet, because they know they're in the public eye."

Are these guys from other countries, or are any of them local

Singapore politicians? She doesn't answer and merely smiles.

"I'll say one thing—sometimes I do get tired of having sex," she laughs, "and I also get tired of pleasing people all the time. That's why for a lot of us girls, things often don't work out in our personal lives and our relationships get wrecked. My boyfriend and I fight a lot because I have higher expectations of him now. A lot of the emotional energy that goes into what I do, that's really the hardest part of this job. The sex is easy.

"It can become so impersonal, when you know it's just a short-time thing and I have felt regret before, especially if the client is cute and he gives me a lot of attention and money. I had one client like that. He was really, really good too, I mean we were rocking the bed and sweating, really sweating! There have been days when I've really wished I could swap my boyfriend for such a man."

"I can get very emotional," she adds. "If I've just had a fight with my boyfriend and I get a call to go meet a client, I will cancel and not go. Because I know I'll get really moody and there will be problems. But most of my clients have been okay, so far. They're not grotesque or anything.

"So, if I think I can still be professional about it, even if I'm in a bad mood, I'll still go ahead," she sighs. She says this standing at a pedestrian crossing on Orchard Road, where the light has just changed from red to green. She walks over to the hotel, her high heels clicking on the asphalt. Condoms are always in her handbag, along with a small leather purse that never says no to more quick cash. "Usually, it really depends on how much I need the money. That's *always* the motivation."

Pizza Delivery

Tall and tawny with lustrous long black hair, Tiffany appears to be everything all Western men seem to want, especially when they're in Asia. She used to laugh about this, a lot more than she does now. Because these days she's somewhat bitter, and perhaps for good reason.

Just where did her good looks get her? She chose her lovely professional name because she liked the connotation of gems and jewellery, of precious things. Of, more precisely, Audrey Hepburn as the fast-talking, smart-mouthed party girl Holly Golightly in *Breakfast at Tiffany's*. Now *that* was the girl she aspired to be! But all this seemed to come undone after she did the ultimate deed, fatefully crossing the line and suddenly creating a living hell for herself that she could scarcely have imagined.

She married one of her customers.

And (drum roll, applause) not just any customer. Frank was a gargantuan limey monster, three hundred pounds of pale, pasty West London flesh, blessed with a bow-legged gait, a double chin and a severely balding head—not exactly in most women's eyes anything close to Jude Law or even Pierce Brosnan (not even in those television spots for L'Oreal anti-wrinkle skin products). But

Frank did have one thing going for him that drew Tiffany like an unsuspecting moth to the flame.

He was rich. Filthy rich. With a filthy mind to match.

His favorite thing was to ask Tiffany to do threesomes with him. He loved to watch two girls get it on while he pulled at his pecker, and just before they'd actually tied the knot he'd bragged to his drinking buddies that he had fucked every single one of Tiffany's girlfriends. Pretty soon, there was only the Filipina maid left but she was a mousy little thing from Lapu-Lapu in Cebu, nothing he'd want to touch with a ten-foot pole.

"Look," he said to his mates whenever he was out with Tiffany. "I'm the oil digger, and she's the gold digger." Frank had made his money on the London IPE (International Petroleum Exchange) and he was amazingly good at speculating on oil futures. He was based in Hong Kong but traveled everywhere, and often spent a lot of time in the United Arab Emirates, where he had an office in Dubai.

The oil digger and the gold digger. At first, Tiffany thought that was funny too.

She prided herself on not taking things all that seriously, especially when she was out with his boozed-up boys, who were all in the oil business too. Some of them worked for the oil refineries offshore, some ran corporations for sheiks in the Gulf states. They were a fun bunch but she only saw them occasionally—because Frank never saw her all that much, unless he was in Singapore on business, and that suited her just fine. They'd already done a fair amount of traveling together, all paid for by Frank, and one afternoon she used his credit card to buy herself a handbag. It was from either Chanel or Gucci, she can't remember which; she only remembers that the price tag was US$20,000. Small change.

She thought this a fair trade. She was living the good life and was trading her beauty and charm to do so. Unbeknown to Frank, she was still escorting and making even more money for herself whenever he wasn't in Singapore. But that was before Frank started getting suspicious, before he hired a private investigator and put him on her tail. She'd married him for his money, and now he wanted to know what his prize catch was up to. He even installed CCTV cameras in every room of the house he had bought her, out in suburban Bukit Timah. Worse still, he even hacked into her email!

It was, to put it mildly, the beginning of the end.

Tiffany bristles at the very thought of him now. "He said to me the other day, 'You should stay with me. Because I'm rich. I can give you the world,'" she hisses. "And I told him, 'Money can't buy happiness. You can buy everything for me, but at the end of the day what I want is the normal things, like a normal guy. I just want a normal guy to be with me, to hug me, to kiss me. If I find the right person, I can give up everything. I don't need someone who is constantly worried and jealous all the time. People ask me, do I seem like a person who likes a lot of drama in her life? Yeah, probably, because it adds a lot of spice to my life. But I don't want this sort of shit. This is fucking way too complicated.

"When I met him, I knew he was rich but I didn't know he was rich rich—not *that* rich! I only found out after a year, when I saw all his business papers and I realized he has millions and millions of dollars, that he's a multimillionaire. The problem now is he knows I was in this line of work, and he can say, 'Look, remember where you came from. I picked you up from this!' He will always say that."

She suddenly looks downcast, much like anyone's idea of the prostitute who is made to feel guilty for her shadowy life and ill-gotten gains. This is why the agency bosses like to tell the girls not to ever marry their clients. Because they'll always have something on you. They'll always be able to blackmail you emotionally and threaten to expose your shameful past.

"No, he doesn't know I've been escorting," she says. "His private investigator was saying to him that I was, and that's why he told me: 'I suspect you've been getting back into your old habits.' But the big one was when he found out about my new boyfriend, who lives in Tokyo. I don't know how he found out. I don't even know what to think anymore. I know for sure that he's insecure and he's having a mid-life crisis. Yeah. Probably. Very insecure. He keeps saying, 'Don't leave me, don't leave me, I don't want to die alone.' He says that's why he married me, so he can have someone always. But it's precisely a double standard. Now he says he's not seeing any escorts anymore so I can't see anyone either.

"And I said, 'What do you mean? When I am faithful to you, what do I get? I get shit!' I reminded him of what happened just two weeks after our so-called marriage. He went to Dubai on business and went for a massage and he had something 'extra' along with the massage. He always tells me this kind of stuff, like he had a 'foam massage' when she covered him with foam and everything and she massaged his 'whole body.' I noticed when he came back, he was so happy. I smelled something wrong. Yeah, he was happy because he'd had a happy ending! I was like, 'What?!! After two weeks of our marriage, you go and do this?!!' And he said, 'What? We weren't fucking. It was just a handjob!' And I said back to him: 'Fuck you! You think that was nothing just because you had a fucking handjob?!! You were messing with somebody else. And she was Russian too!'"

How did all this happen? Ask her that and she just shakes her head in abject dismay.

"When I met him, I thought, he's stable—financially—and I thought well, I won't have to worry about my life, because he's going to look after me and everything," she sighs. "And, of course, I admit I thought that, well, he's old and he's going to die anyway, and hopefully quite soon." She laughs, as if caught out by the sheer irony of those words.

"I mean, I'm twenty-seven and he's sixty! Can you believe that?!!" She throws her hands up in the air. "I found that when I was with him, the age gap *did* make quite a difference, especially to our conversations. Our topics are always just about old men's stuff—old, old movies and things I can't relate to at all. He would talk about music and I've never heard of all these people. I think it's too late for me to learn about all this. I mean, his favorite singers are Perry Como and Peggy Lee. I had no idea who they were. I thought Peggy Lee was a local TV actress on Channel 8."

Things didn't get much better at all when Frank discovered she'd acquired a new beau behind his back. "Yes, when I met my new guy, my American guy in Tokyo, the one I fell in love with, well, he's only thirty-five and it was easier," Tiffany explains. "I don't always like older men, but I have been with younger guys before and it's always just so hard because they can't even support themselves, and I'm not going to support them. I've done that once and I'm not that stupid anymore.

"In the beginning, I just thought it was a one-night stand, especially since he lives in Tokyo. So I didn't make a real effort to get to know him. But I have a soft spot for guys who can play guitar and sing, and he did that for me and I was—gone! He played my favorite song, "Yellow" by Coldplay, and I was so touched and I was just crazy for him. I realized I was falling for him and we kept in touch by email. He didn't know what I really did for a living, he thought I was just modeling. But now he knows. I told him everything, and he's okay with it. Actually, we met when I was escorting in Tokyo—I'd been flown out there by a client!"

Well, the modeling bit was not entirely a lie. She was a catalog and occasional television-advert model, having done a nice shampoo commercial that unfortunately ran only in the Philippines. The work, however, was much too sporadic and she wasn't always employed. When she started escorting, she knew that her good looks would get her past any hotel room door quite easily, even though she wasn't too sure at first. The fact that she's of Eurasian descent was, in some ways, an asset—her father is Chinese and her mother is Dutch—and some Asian guys really get turned on when they know a girl is half-white. And the Caucasian guys like the Asian side of her. It seems like such a win-win thing.

Tiffany enjoys projecting the "bad girl" image anyway. When she started modeling at age nineteen, she smoked and drank and kept late hours with the best of them, and her lovely face wore nary a visible sign of wear or tear. It was pretty good going for those first few years. "Back then I had a lot of credit cards, and my mom was not well and she fell sick. She's since passed away, but I paid for some of her medical bills and used up my credit cards for that. So I was starting to pay back what I owed, and then I was with this younger guy and I was paying for everything. When you love somebody, you tend to do all this silly stuff, you know, but then I learned I owed the banks big time—more than S$100,000. So I began thinking, shoot, what am I going to do? Every week, every month, I have more and more stuff to pay for! I can't keep modeling—it's not enough. I got into escorting because of the prospect of the money I could make."

She found her agency from, of all places, a local tabloid called *The New Paper*. "I wasn't sure if it would work, because I didn't know what to expect, but I decided I would at least try it once. I saw this classified ad and so I sent my picture to them and then I received a call to go in for an interview. I panicked and didn't know what to do! I didn't even know where that address was. When I arrived, I was asked to fill in the form and I overheard the lady tell another girl about the job and what the scope of the job was and what was involved. Then it was my turn and I remember we talked about the payment scheme and about what I felt comfortable with. I told her I wasn't interested in doing any 'extra' work, I just wanted to do this for dinner or just to go shopping. I just told her straight.

"And she said, 'Sure, you can do that, but there's always a better way to get more money.' I told her I wasn't comfortable with that, and she said, 'Fine, why don't you think about it? Meantime we'll just put you down as a social escort.' I said okay. And then after two days of thinking, I called and I said, 'Fine, I'll try it and I'll see how it works out for me.' Now I think back and I see how funny that was. I think that if you do this not wanting to do the 'extras' then it really doesn't work, because the job *is* the 'extras'!"

By sheer happenstance, she lucked out. Her very first client was kind and understanding. "He was really, really nice. We didn't do anything, we just sat around talking. I was so nervous, you know, because he was my first one. I told him that and he seemed to understand. He booked me overnight too, so maybe that scared me, knowing I would almost certainly have to sleep with him till the morning.

"But he was amazing—he paid me the full overnight rate even though I left much earlier, because I told him I needed to get home to rest. We spent five hours together. He paid me S$1,000 and even told me to buy shoes at Takashimaya. He told me to go to this shoe shop there and buy whatever shoes I liked, just give them his name and it's all paid for. So I did, I went and got my shoes. Of course, I found an expensive pair! Well, not the *most* expensive pair there, but certainly the most beautiful. I will always remember him for that."

Intoxicated by this change of fortune, she decided this line of work was more than agreeable with her. She was lucky indeed— S$1,000 and a new pair of Manolo Blahniks, and she didn't even have to fuck the guy! She could hardly believe it. Were there more guys like this one out there?

Yes, there were. But not after her first client was done with her. "What happened was, he supported me for a year," Tiffany discloses. "Every month without fail, he would transfer S$1,000 into my bank account, which helped me to pay my bills. And in that whole year, I only had sex with him once. He's a busy man, quite a well-known person—I cannot reveal his identity. He's not Singaporean but comes here a lot. Anyway, he finally asked me to stop escorting but I told him I could not, because I still had to pay off my loans. I told him it was too early for me to do that.

"After the fifth month, however, it became kind of a pain in the ass, because I had to call him every time to ask him to transfer money. He kept saying he forgot to transfer it. He's no longer in my life now—he invited me to a big gala event and then at the last minute, he was a no-show. He never even called me, not at all. I finally got hold of him and told him not to ever promise me anything, because I felt like leaving. And then, after that, we just lost contact."

But by that time, a whole year had lapsed and Tiffany was already a seasoned pro. She became one of the most in-demand girls at the agency. Her overnight bookings were frequent and she also received a lot of requests for threesomes, which she would often perform with her friend Shakira, an Indian girl, and they would always meet at the designated hotel and head straight for the bathroom to freshen up before going up to the room, chatting about the craziness of the business. ("To a lot of these guys, it's like we're delivering pizza," Shakira once told her. "Only instead of pizza, we're delivering pussy. Yeah, our pussies bring food to the table!") They were a fearsome twosome, because they both had no qualms about the demands of their profession.

"The idea of my job being so tied to sex, that's fine if I do it with someone I like," Tiffany says. "I really enjoy it. I don't mind doing it every day. And going to a hotel to meet some guy I've never met before, I don't mind it too, actually. I do still have that feeling, that desire to explore the unknown, I like it. And for a few reasons too. Firstly, the money is easy, and secondly, I get to see different people. I like variety. It spices up my life, it spices up my sex. With some guys you give them a blowjob, with other guys you do other things, and there's no strings attached. I'm naturally sexual. I love sex. I confessed to Frank that, sorry, I cannot just stick to one guy."

"I even have a small vibrator, shaped like a lipstick," she adds. "It's like a 'pocket rocket' and I always keep it in my make-up pouch. And the other day, a friend of mine wanted to use my makeup and she took it out and she went, 'What is this?!!' I said, 'It's mine, stop touching it!' and everyone was laughing. I tell them, 'When I get bored, if I'm waiting for something or someone, I just use it.' It goes on my clit. I have seven of them now, plus this small little one, so that's eight. I don't use them that much though. I would rather have a guy with me. The thing with self-pleasure is that I can control it, and when the time comes I do that and that's it. I'm not addicted to it. But if I have a man, I don't mind doing it every day."

The clients do come in all shapes and sizes, though, and one incident still makes her shudder. "I had this huge client. He was so fat and I remember thinking, the first time I saw him, 'I'm doing to die! He's going to be on top of me and I'm going to get squashed like a bug!' It turned out that he was so fat we couldn't do anything other than a handjob, which is what I gave him. His penis was small—very, very small—and I almost cried when I saw it. A lot of times, because they're so fat, they can't even come. He was really huge. That's why I thought I was going to die, 'cos what else could we do, you know? Anyway, that was the one and only time I was with him. As I was leaving he actually said to me: 'The next time I'm in Singapore with my wife, let's have a threesome.' And I said, 'Are you kidding?!!'

"Look, I'm good at what I do. I will moan and groan and whatever, aloud, but I really need to enjoy it. But if I was doing it every day with someone like my husband Frank, I'd get sick of it. Because he's not attractive, he's old, he's fat and he's slow—it takes a long time for him to come and everything. For me, it's like, 'Oh, c'mon, Frank, get it over and done with!' I always want a quickie with him, but it can't ever be a quickie, you know. It takes at least half an hour. And then I'll be like really tired and then I have to rush to work, and all that. When I first met him, I didn't think he would want to have sex with me every day, like every morning and every night! I think that's okay if you like it, but the problem is I get sick of it. When he's on top of me and he's sweating and stuff, sweating on me, and I hate it when it gets on my face! Sometimes he smells bad, a little. Not *bad* bad but there's an odor."

She snorts her nose in disgust and shrugs her shoulders in defeat. "Honestly, if not for that situation, I would have stopped escorting altogether. I've been doing this for two years and the excitement that I felt at the start is now gone. Now, I meet these men and I know that's all they really want. All the conversation and the dinner, all that is just bullshit. It's difficult at times when you have a regular client and you start to have feelings for him. I've had that happen a few times. There are a few that I'm still in contact with right now and we're still really close. But I don't think I can fall in love with a 'normal' person. It would be pretty difficult, actually, because you already have another life and you're always worried that he's going to find out or if he's checking on you, which is already happening to me. I think if I cool off for a while, it will be okay. It's really a big problem for me because I'm a woman and I still want to have that feeling of love. Sometimes you fall in love with somebody who is not in this line of work, and that's a different scenario, because my thing is I don't want him to know. So I live a double life.

"Even with my friends, they're always asking me where I'm going, why I am always leaving to go somewhere else at the last minute when I'm out with my friends, why I'm always saying 'Sorry, guys, I gotta go,' and then I'm rushing off somewhere. And

47

my dressing is really different from theirs, it's really super-nice, and they're wondering just where exactly I'm going. You can't wear jeans in this job. Sometimes, I dress down but I'll bring my dress with me, I always wear heels so it's not a problem. It's very rare that I'll be out wearing sports attire. I always bring extra clothes and stuff. So I tell them I have to 'meet people.' But when it happens too often, they'll be thinking why I'm going, or why I keep being gone sometimes for three days at a time."

To allay her husband's suspicions, she actually stopped working for a whole month, though the boyfriend in Tokyo was still a well-kept secret. "I've actually stopped. At this point, anyway. The money is good and there are no strings attached and I like it. But because I am attached, or so-called attached, now and with the tight security that I have, I have decided to cool off for a while. But if you ask me, honestly, I would rather continue to do it rather than be attached to somebody who is like spot-checking on me and all that. Doing it with no strings attached, rather than being with somebody who is always asking: 'Where is the money that I gave you?' They will say they are supporting you but they want something back in return. He bought me this massive house in Bukit Timah, which is where I live now, but now he's put cameras in all the rooms and I even discovered that my personal email has been hacked into! What kind of husband would do that to his wife?!!"

She pauses, grabs a tissue, and starts to cry.

"Yeah, I have to leave him at some point," she sobs. "How much more complicated can my life be? I just want a normal life. It's getting worse, and you know what I want to do? I want to get him out of my life and just start all over again. But it's not easy to leave him. He's invested money in my company—we started a modeling agency together—and he can take the shares from my company. Now I know why he's not married to this day. Look what he's doing to me! I'd heard from one of his friends that this has happened before, with another girl. I don't know the details. He was supposed to get married two years before, to a South African girl, and the girl said she didn't want to get married. I wonder why."

Her cellphone suddenly beeps. A text message from the agency. There's a job for her. Two Arabs are in town and they want her and Shakira to tag-team again. "Damn! Usually, when I'm really busy and I know I don't have time, I just don't answer the phone. Then it's like this, you know, 'Be at such-and-such hotel at eight o'clock!' There was a time when I was working as a mascot—modeling as a brand mascot at an event in a shopping mall—and my agency boss called me. I told her I was doing mascot work and she asked me how much I was getting paid for it. I told her 'Seventy dollars' and she said, 'Seventy bucks? For seventy bucks, you're doing this?' And I said, 'Yeah, well, at least I don't have to open my legs!' She didn't think that was funny. She said, 'You should come here and get more.' And I said, 'Yes, but that's going to take at least three hours. Here, I see children and I make them happy and they like to see me. I make more people happy and not just one person—one person with too much money!'"

She shrugs again. She seems to be doing that a lot these days.

And the Arabs are waiting.

She calls Shakira.

"Fuck Frank," she murmurs under her breath. "At least I'll have her for company. Some guys are kinky and want to see us eat each other out. Well, I've eaten her before and she's not bad at all. It's better than doing a blowjob. At least I know what she tastes like. She's my best friend and you don't get this happening in the real world, where you and your best friend work together like this."

She suddenly breaks into a grin. These Arabs aren't going to rescue her from her misery but it'll be a nice change from Frank and his madness. Even though she knows she's merely treading water. Wealthy men are like sharks, sniffing for blood. Well, too late, she's already put herself on the auction block.

She's off to meet Shakira. They're soul sisters. They're going to deliver pizza again. With all the toppings and extra cheese too. And they're going to make bank.

"*You should stay with me. Because I'm rich. I can give you the world.*"

"*Look, remember where you came from. I picked you up*

from this!"

Frank's just going to love the smell on her when she gets home tonight.

Hit Press and Play

The girl on the dance floor at Zouk could be anyone, and nobody would ever guess her profession. She shimmers as if in some psychedelic trance as Madonna's "Ray of Light" starts to play, and there's just a trace of sex in her movements, just enough to make any hot-blooded male take notice. Shakira, who named herself after the sexy Colombian singer (and certainly has the hips to match), says most of her clients are "average"—most of them tend to come pretty quickly, in single-minded pursuit of that so-called "happy ending."

Men are all the same, she scoffs, and wishes it could be more enjoyable for her. But she knows that's not why she's an escort—personal satisfaction isn't the same as job satisfaction, not in this business. The girl is always there to service the guy and give him what he wants. Her own needs aren't part of the equation. She's just a live warm body for them to gawk and grope, like some newfangled gadget they've acquired for their own amusement. Just hit press and play.

It all started when her mother threw her out of the house after learning that her only daughter had lost her virginity. She was fifteen then (and a normal teenager, for crying out loud) but the old crone, her very own mother, called her a slut, a whore, an unclean thing. What kind of young girl had she raised, after all they'd done to become a good Singaporean Indian family?

She went back home and tried to look chastened but it didn't work. Her mother made her life a living hell. She wasn't allowed to go out and she wasn't allowed to have friends. "Nobody in the world loves me," she sobbed. Well, her father did, but he was long gone, having walked out on the family back when she was nine years old.

She's been looking for a father figure ever since, but without much success. True, there were countless older men who would zip in and out of her life, their zippers very much undone, but what these middle-aged guys didn't understand was that they were merely vehicles for the expression of her sublimated rage. She was angry with her mother and father for abandoning her, and with the boy in school who'd popped her cherry and then acted as if they'd never ever met.

That had really hurt. These men, they would collectively pay. Her profession as an escort is really her way of enacting sweet, savage metaphysical revenge.

Money is what she needs right now, and she knows just how to get it—to attain the maximum reward for the minimum outlay, so to speak—and sometimes she laughs at the fools who think they can own her for just a few hours. Men, she thinks, are such idiots.

Sometimes, she wonders, why do they even bother? Any idiot can go to a hotel bar and pick up a sweet young thing who can be charmed out of her clothes without having to be bought with cold hard cash. "I actually asked one of my clients this," she reveals, "a really nice, good-looking American guy who was here on business. He was quite cute, actually. He'd be great boyfriend material except, of course, I'll never date him now. Anyway, he said he couldn't afford to be seen in public trying to pick up a girl. He's a high-level corporate executive with a very big company and so he needs to be more discreet. Besides, he told me, when he lands in Singapore, he wants to be able to pick up the phone and dial. Instant gratification! He was just here in Singapore last week, in fact, and I ran into him by accident at a restaurant on Boat Quay. He asked if I could go with him and I said no, because I was having my period. And you know what he said? He was, like, 'Oh, okay. Well, uh, I'll call for you the next time I'm in Singapore then. See you later.' And that was it!

"I was so—I don't know what the word is—embarrassed? Humiliated? Or maybe I was just terribly disappointed. I mean, he was so blunt about what he wanted me for. Like, he had no interest in taking me out to lunch or coffee or dinner or anything like that, he only wanted me for one thing. And if I couldn't provide that one thing that week, it was like, 'Forget it, see you next time.' You know what I mean? I don't remember this ever happening to me, not this way—being told point blank I'm just useful to him for sex, that I am basically just a prostitute. He was so sweet to me the last time we were together, and I even kissed him. He told me, 'Oh, I thought you girls don't kiss. Back in the States, they all don't.' And I said, 'Well, if I want to kiss someone, I just go ahead and do so. That's how I am.' And now I can't believe what a fool I was, to think I could actually like this guy. He paid me S$1,000 and he was sort of average, had a small dick and came too fast, but I could see us being friends, you know. Now I see I was just being naive."

Her naïveté might've been due to her ingenue status as an escort. She's eighteen going on nineteen and has been working the swanky hotels in Singapore for just about one year. Prior to that, she worked as a hostess in a KTV bar, where she was the only Indian girl. There was a *mamasan* there named Nicole, who was very kind to her, even though they never worked directly together; Shakira worked for some of the other *mamasan*s, who didn't have to do much to make her brown-skinned ethnicity stand out like a class brand among the bevy of mainland Chinese girls who looked so very pale in comparison.

But four months there, and she was out. It was just too much, having to be there every night of the week, drinking hard liquor and then having to do unmentionable things for money. She was born a good Hindu, after all, even if she was certainly less than devout. "I only had sex with five guys there in all that time, seriously," she recalls. "I really wasn't into them at all, these loud, rude and uncouth Chinese businessmen, and I thought I'd better get the hell out of there before I go crazy. These China girls were doing blowjobs without condoms, can you imagine that? Nicole was the one who actually suggested I go see the escort agency I'm with now. She didn't mind me leaving the club and said I should do what's best for me. I loved dancing with the guys, because I naturally love to dance, but all the hard liquor and late nights were really starting to kill me."

The money at the KTV club wasn't bad. For a one-time session, it was S$400 for a "short-time" quickie, not inclusive of the *mamasan*'s fee. "So I took about S$300, and then long-time it was anything from S$600 to S$800. Depending on the *mamasan*, if she was good. For long-time, I kept S$600. The trick, though, was to find ways to keep yourself outside the club without telling the *mamasan*, like the guys would tell me they didn't want to take me because they were too drunk, and then they would meet me privately at the hotel or wherever and pay me more. Or sometimes what they'd do is we'd sit together in very close proximity, so as soon as it was agreed we would leave separately and not let the *mamasan* know and meet outside, elsewhere. To this day, I think Nicole doesn't know I did this, but I didn't actually work with her and never slept with any of her clients, anyway. It's just a fun thing we hostesses do to keep our lives interesting, I guess."

Was the change of pace going to be as interesting? She went to the agency with a mixture of excitement and fear.

On one hand, she thought of it like graduating, up one level in the sex worker food chain. There was a sense of secrecy, since she didn't have to be seen in as public a place as a KTV club, where the girls pretty much openly advertised themselves as sluts for hire. No, being an escort, that was a lot more classy. Like Catherine Deneuve in her celebrated role of the devoted *haute bourgeois* wife who secretly works at an upmarket brothel in Luis Bunuel's classic film *Belle de Jour*—now that had a decadent ring to it that she liked.

She'd done some reading on the profession and she knew the score. The etymology of the word "pornography" means "the writings of prostitutes," she'd learned, and the reason behind this stunned her. Historically, prostitutes who worked in brothels made money on volume—the more clients they saw, the more money they made—so they took to writing sexual stuff and posting sexual photographs on the walls of their rooms in order to speed up the process. Their clients would be more turned-on when they saw the sexually explicit words and pictures, and this meant that they got down to business and finished faster.

"Most men just want to come and get it down and over with," Shakira says, in solidarity with her sisters of yore. "Makes it easier for the rest of us." The other girls at the agency often laugh at her, sitting in a corner reading a book while the rest of them chat and gossip while waiting for clients to arrive. The waiting is a real pain, but they are there because the men have made appointments or want to see some girls first before choosing their companion for the night. Shakira would rather be elsewhere, so she can let the phone ring. Her Nokia cellphone is her most valuable possession. "When you're an escort, you're constantly on call and that's why some people call us call girls," she surmises, "since we live and die by our cellphones."

She was actually out at a dance club one night when it rang and she had to exit, hastily making some excuse to her friends about a "family emergency" and racing off to get a taxi. There was a gentleman waiting for her in his hotel suite. "I finished at 8 a.m. the next morning. This was November 2007, I remember it well. He booked me from 11 p.m. to 7 a.m. but convinced me to stay an hour longer, paid me S$1,600—of which I keep S$1,000 and the agency gets S$600. He's an Indian-born CEO of a computer sales company, and his family have enormous holdings all across Asia, so he flies back and forth a lot, and lives part of the year in California, in Silicon Valley. He was actually very nice. I'd brought two condoms in my handbag and we used both! One for the blowjob and one on his cock for my pussy, and he even whipped out a vibrator to use on me. It was really big! But I enjoyed it."

It's always the best job when someone is nice enough to make sure she enjoys herself too, but that guy is often the exception and not the norm. She isn't crazy about most of them—there have been too many evenings when she has had to indulge in small talk or sit in the room watching TV while the client is on the phone trying to finish up a business call. "I had a Greek shipping guy who made me watch TV pretty much all night while he was on the phone. After he hung up, he told me he was too tired to do anything else and wanted to go to sleep, so he paid me to leave. He paid me the overnight rate—the whole S$1,600, and apologized and asked if I didn't mind leaving. Wow, I thought, was this guy kidding? I got a thousand bucks and didn't have to fuck him, so of course I was happy!"

But was it really money for nothing? What would she have done more usefully with those hours that she'd spent watching *American Idol* and *Fear Factor* in his hotel room? She shrugs. Every job comes with occupational hazards and that one was the least harmful. It wasn't like getting a sexually transmitted disease, which was a whole lot worse. Shakira had contracted chlamydia twice, and one of those was from doing a threesome and going down on the other girl "who smelled a bit funny down there."

But maybe that is a hazard about being bisexual, not just about escorting. She likes having a job that allows her to express her sexuality. Being paid for it is supposedly a bonus. "We do provide a useful service and I don't see why I should hate myself for being a sex object," she says. "I see the pragmatism in why society needs sex objects and discreet services, at the same time being aware that it is only an illusion and they too are people." The fact that she can even articulate her thoughts like this makes her a constant favorite among the Caucasians who use her agency.

"They tend to be rather talkative themselves and like to have a girl who can have a real conversation," she notes. "For me, strangely, I've been in this business almost a year but I've never slept with an Asian guy. Never have. Even out of this line of work, I've never actually dated an Asian guy. I don't like them. I know I'm stereotyping here, even though I'm Asian myself, but they're a little too chauvinistic and a little too controlling. I don't like that. I've heard stories from some of the other Asian girls who do this to support their boyfriends and I just don't believe in that. Selling your body to support a boyfriend? I think those girls are just so stupid."

Shakira took a deferment from her studies—she's a finance major and wants to be an investment banker someday—in order to make extra money right after she left her mother's home for good. "What I really need is my permanent pool of clients," she laughs. "I only have four regular clients now. A few more sugar daddies, that's what I need and life would be much better. Ha ha! I've been very lucky. I've never been mistreated in any way. The agency's clients are mostly respectable men who just want companions. There have been a few times when I have felt afraid, and what I do is try to have it arranged so we go out in a group and I'll be standoffish, especially if they get too drunk, so they won't really like me and they'll tell me to go home.

"I know of one girl who was actually *raped* by a client! She told me all about it. He was very rough and she told him to stop and he wouldn't and just forced himself into her, harder and harder, and she was crying. But the guy is one of the more regular clients at the agency so she didn't complain. She decided it was no use and just never accepted a job involving that guy again."

What recourse did an escort have in complaining about being raped? That was like a football player griping about hard tackles and ankle injuries, all those risks that naturally came with the choice of profession. Shakira has lots of stories about weird things that have happened to her on the job. "I had this one guy who couldn't, you know, couldn't keep it up. He was really young and I wasn't really sure what to do. I mean, I tried to help him. I masturbated him and he couldn't do it. And then he started crying. He cried and cried and, as it turned out, he had some issues about his personal life. I got him stressed out and so I had to soothe him. Sometimes in this job, you have to do this with people. In the end, he was just crying, and I just gave him a kiss. No sex.

"The weirdest one was this guy who wanted me to pee on him and he wanted to drink it too. Not a Japanese guy, like you would think. He was Italian. So I did it anyway, in a bathtub. He had his mouth, you know, down my pubic area and I peed and everything went in." Did the guy gulp down all her juicy goodness? "I suppose so. I can't imagine why anyone would want to do that! He paid the normal rate and then he saw that I was afraid at first and so he said he would pay me more. There was another guy who liked me to pinch and play with his nipples with my fingers. And as we were making love, he kept shouting out, 'My wife would never do this to me!' That was a bit bizarre.

"They always ask me if I will do 'extra' for extra money and what I charge them depends on what the 'extra' is. I had one guy who didn't want to use a condom. It really felt strange, with all the risks involved, and he told me he'd pay something extra and asked me to get a check-up after that and if there was anything wrong to tell him and he would pay my medical bills!"

Did she do it? "Yeah, I did it. But that was my first and only time. I would never do that again. The risks are too high. I did it because he was offering me quite good money—S$1,000 just to do that, even though it was only a short-time booking. I've been lucky so far. No whipping or spanking or sodomizing yet. The kinkiest thing I've done is a threesome, with another girl and the guy, which I like because I am bisexual. I am attracted to girls. I've never had a girl client but I have been a client for a girl—I used to have a boyfriend who was into three-way sex and we would go to clubs in Tanjong Pagar to find girls. I have this weird thing—I like seeing him having sex with another girl. It really turns me on, watching him fuck her. Also, having been in this business I've become quite desensitized to sex with men and actually get more pleasure being with a woman."

She broke up with him recently, and the entire time they were together he had no clue whatsoever that she was escorting. "That was right after I left the KTV job and I was a freelance dancer at some nightclubs, doing some part-time work, so every time I had to do this, I told him I was out working late. In that line of work, you have to be early for rehearsals and there's a lot of stage work and so I had to be gone for long periods of time. He understood. He didn't ever control what I did and, as far as I know, he never checked my cellphone.

"At first I felt bad but I wasn't dating him for long, we were only together for four months. He's Australian, from Tasmania, and he wanted to return to Hobart anyway. We split up when he told me he was in love with someone else, and I guess it was my own retribution, since I wasn't totally faithful to him."

"Even though, technically," she insists, "this is only just a job."

However, the job was fast becoming more than merely that. It was metamorphosing into a whole way of life for her. The dance jobs had dried up and the school deferment meant she had no other way of making ends meet, especially since there was no fat-cat big-cheese boyfriend to pay for her meals and her entertainment, and she was now living alone in her own apartment out on the East Coast, in the gentrified boondocks of darkest Siglap.

Well, she thought, she could've been in Punggol or Simei, in the Housing-Development-Board heartland, which would've been a living death. There was now this lifestyle that she had become accustomed to, and it was just too hard to give up.

"I also started thinking about how most of my clients are usually older men who have fantasies about having sex with a much younger woman, much younger than their wives," she reflects. "Then there's the thing about having no strings attached. They can find a young girl elsewhere but she would probably just want him for his money and all that, and when emotions get involved that gets too complicated. Some men want things they can't get from their spouses, so we're their resource. And for some men who hit that mid-life crisis, they want to feel appreciated and maybe their wives don't have the same attractiveness they used to have twenty or thirty years ago and they hope then to get that from a younger woman. I really see it as a pragmatic thing, because we both need something.

"Also, I am a very sexual person. I only realized the full extent of this after I got into this business. Before, I wasn't really exposed to men like this. I suppose how it started was, before I started doing this I had this thing against men mostly because of a few spurned lovers. I think the very first time I had a one-night stand, I felt very liberated—knowing that I can actually do that, get involved with someone I don't even know and at the same time not feel a thing after that, even immediately after that. I can be very emotional and I can be attracted to someone very easily, so when I realized I could do that it made me feel like there was this thing in me that was like a rage against men, inside. After that, I realized that was how I could do this, without feeling.

"I have heard stories from other girls, about how it was horrible and how they didn't like it, but it wasn't the case with me. I think now that it was so valuable that I had my first one-night stand outside the business, before I started escorting. So I knew I could do this. To me it was like something that *had* to be done. Once it was over, it meant I had something that would last me for a few days, if it was paying for school fees or paying for bills, you know. I always think of the objective, and keep it in mind."

But she knows her days will be numbered in a year or two, and she needs to make hay while her sun shines. "My boss at the agency, he actually said to me: 'If you want to stay here for a long time, it's bad. It's bad for you because you should only be here because you're in a condition in your life whereby you need something desperately. But don't make this something permanent. Don't do this because you've decided the money is so good that you're going to do this for the rest of your life.'

"I think that was so amazing of him to say that. He gives that same advice to all the girls. I mean, right now I'm working three or four times a week, but there are days when you can have two or three calls. It all depends on the business. It can be really quiet at times. That's the difference between this and the KTV clubs. When I was a KTV girl, I could go there every day, or rather every night, and I was bound to get people. Whereas with this, sometimes they might not call you. So being a KTV girl is more steady work. I would've kept doing it if I could deal with the environment. I had to take a school deferment to work there since it was daily work, so I'm now kind of stuck.

"The thing is, I could work at a bar as a waitress but I had to get my own apartment and the thing about me is I get used to a certain lifestyle. I wouldn't know how to live just to make ends meet. Living to get by day by day, working as a waitress when they pay you so little."

The option to return to the *karaoke* nightlife isn't negotiable, she says, even when the *mamasan*s from her old job still call her with offers. "Yeah, the *mamasan*s still call me to say they have foreign customers, especially Caucasians, and they need me because I can speak English. Most of the Chinese girls there can't speak English. I do speak Mandarin a bit, but my place there was for the guys who wanted something different and the *mamasan* would go, 'Oh, we have a local girl if you want.' It's a big advantage for me! But what happens if I run into someone I know? I know KTV is a Chinese thing but some foreigners do go and if I see them there, like one of my ex-boyfriend's expat friends, that wouldn't be such a good thing."

Her long-term goal is to finish school somehow. "I plan to graduate and get a real job," she laughs. "Yeah, I know, a 'real job.' We'll see. Life is never easy when you're starting a career and I'm still young. The thing with this business is that you start getting paid quite a bit, so there's no such thing as a 'real job' that pays you like this. This is something I have had to come to terms with. The only thing is I get sick of having sex sometimes. It really has become a job to me and I'm getting bored with it, with these guys and their silly problems. To think that you can fix your problems by buying a woman, for a temporary thrill. I really think these men are such losers."

She pauses. The crowd at Zouk is thinning now, it's way past anyone's bedtime. There's nobody she sees that she'd even consider going home with.

"It makes me wonder," she says, "if I can ever have a real boyfriend anymore. I'm not sure how it would feel to have sex with someone you really love, when I'm always having sex for work. And I'm not even nineteen yet! Is that sad or what?"

PART TWO

Dates with Delusion

The Fishbowls
and the Four Floors

The exotic allure of the sexually available Asian woman, he had heard, was quite something else. A phenomenon he had to experience at least once in his lifetime. Singapore, he was told, had some really beautiful women, and some of them were surely for sale. Like the ones in Thailand, who were legendary for their prowess in the ways of the erotic arts.

That's what Jeffrey Kaminsky thought, anyway, just before he made the trip out to Southeast Asia from his home in Los Angeles, California.

Jeffrey considers himself to be the quintessential sex tourist, having previously savored the pleasures of the flesh in the brothels of Argentina, Brazil, Germany, and other points hither and yon. He declares Stiletto in Sydney, Australia, the "best brothel in the world, bar none," though he also likes the infamous FKK Club in Germany, where a black Jamaican girl sucked his cock in open view of everyone. Ah, she knew just what to do—her mouth was all slurpy with her saliva, and boy did it feel good.

Southeast Asia was virgin territory to him, though, and it would be his first time in these parts. Jeff had heard so much about the girls in Thailand that he decided he would head for Bangkok, with a brief pit stop in the Lion City. Someone had told him about the red-light district of Geylang, so he decided he would try his luck. He particularly wanted to see Lorong 16, famous for its "fishbowls"—those houses equipped with "aquariums" where petite Thai girls waited patiently behind plate-glass partitions with numbers fastened to their skimpy dresses.

How apropos, he thought, that each of them was reduced to being just a number. He'd also heard about Orchard Towers, the shopping mall on Orchard Road, which underwent a fascinating transformation each night, turning into the fabled "four floors" (as in "four floors of whores," as the local joke goes). How could he possibly resist all this?

"I was impressed at how tidy and clean everything was," he now says of Geylang in general. "And how well behaved the male clients were. Also, how few men were actually cruising the streets. At the end of the streets, it was more what I was used to elsewhere—milling crowds of prowling males, some out to buy, most out to look—but on the *lorongs* themselves, there was almost no one."

Ah, but he'd gone there on one of the quieter nights, though as a matter of course there never is a big din about Geylang. It may well be the best-behaved red-light district in the world, providing service with a smile in the most orderly manner, ever so redolent of Singapore's squeaky-clean public image.

"Every other commercial sex district I've visited, it's all about having a lone brothel among restaurants, stores, and other commercial interests, so people don't congregate—there's nothing to see unless you go inside," he discloses. "The only actual red-light districts I can compare Geylang to are those in Amsterdam and Tijuana, Mexico. Both are filled with men walking up and down the streets, looking for someone who piques their sexual curiosity and whets their appetites. And in both areas the men tend to be loud and abrasive. Fights or confrontations are not uncommon. One of my most treasured memories comes from Tijuana, when one guy came flying out from between the swinging saloon doors to land on his back in the street, with the bouncer close on his heels. It was like a scene out of a John Ford Western movie! That was very much like what the saloons of the American West were like a little over a hundred years ago."

Well, he certainly wasn't in the old American West anymore, but he found Geylang somewhat different from what he'd expected. "Unlike most red-light districts I've been to, Geylang is a pleasant, modest, middle-class neighborhood with a few conspicuous medium-rise hotels. Everything is neat and clean and well tended. It's a far cry from most commercial sex zones in the West, or even Thailand for that matter. No bars or clubs with loud music, garish lights, and giddy frivolity. But this was definitely sex for the masses, since I didn't see too many Benzes or Bentleys parked on the streets."

At one of the "aquarium" houses on Lorong 16, he chose Number 9. Indeed, like all the other girls, she wore her number pinned to her dress, so any customer could indicate his choice without rudely pointing at her. He laughed when he saw a sign on the wall warning patrons that they would be made to leave the premises should the girls ever discover penis studs or any other metallic genital ornamentation. (Jeff didn't have a cock ring or anything impaling his dick, but what were they going to do, make him drop his pants for inspection first?)

Number 9 was a tall, tanned Thai beauty from Chiang Mai. Her name, she told him with no obvious sarcasm, was "Star." Jeff was six foot two, so he liked the fact that this girl was taller than some of the others, and he was all smiles when she took him upstairs to perform her duty. He was paying her S$80 for forty minutes.

The next morning, he described the encounter as "the single worst sexual experience" of his whole life.

She wouldn't blow him "bareback" (meaning without a condom) and she wouldn't do certain positions and she wouldn't use any lube even though she was rather dry and she wouldn't even summon the enthusiasm to help him finish. Instead, she kept moaning that time was running out and they needed to complete the task before the buzzer went off at the forty-minute mark.

What a clock-watcher! And what a letdown!

Undeterred, he went the next evening to Orchard Towers, where he chatted up a pretty Vietnamese girl. She went back with him to his hotel, and gave him what he later declared "an even worse experience" than his Geylang misadventure.

"Her name was My Lai, as in the massacre," he said grumpily, which pretty much said it all.

He was astounded—he had struck out two nights in a row, after all the wonderful things he had heard about the whores of Singapore. And after all the Viagra he had taken too. The little blue pills were obviously no match for the girls' lack of enthusiasm. Sex between consenting adults is necessarily an interactive activity, and those girls didn't really want to interact.

"My Thai girl was very friendly on the floor, but once we got upstairs, her mood changed," he said. "Had I been able to chat with her for a bit, I probably could have picked up a reticence. I think the 'aquarium' is a good system in that it saves the embarrassment of pointing to someone and you can ask what she will and will not do. On the other hand, there's something to be said about one-on-one conversation and the feeling you get in your gut about a girl. I didn't get the chance to do this with her since we had no conversation at all before we went upstairs to the room."

"My first disappointment, actually, was the room itself," he remembers. "It was cramped, with a small shower in the corner.

But most distressing was the lack of mirrors. I mean, this was a whorehouse, right? And any brothel worth its salt has mirrors on at least a couple of walls. When I asked the girl where were the mirrors, she said: 'Why?' I said: 'To watch,' and she gave me a puzzled look.

"I was starting to get nervous. We showered, then got on the bed. Things progressed according to the book—no passion, no spark, but adequate. I got a covered blowjob, and we did some spanking and squeezing, and it was only when we started to fuck that things got a little iffy."

Iffy? Which rhymes with 'jiffy'? As in, she wanted it done quickly? "Well, we began with missionary, which is not my favorite position," he explains, "but it was okay for starters. As I picked up steam, she began to complain that I was going 'too deep,' and that I was 'too long.' Hmm. I recognized this as a ploy from 'Whore Tactics 101' to cut the session short—a classic attempt to slow things down and not give me my money's worth. I ignored her and continued to go balls-deep, despite her moans and cries of protest. When I suggested we change positions, she was reluctant but agreed if I wouldn't go as deep. She was going, 'You're too long. It's painful.'"

He pauses and laughs. "Hey, I'm not John Holmes, but I'm not burdened with shrinkage problems either. During my visit to a Bangkok brothel, I noticed that Asian pussies are shallower than the Western version, but both girls can accommodate me without effort, and neither complained about my length or vigor or stamina. Singapore, clearly, is different—more conservative, less emphasis on Olympic sex and more on just getting the client off and out. Anyway, with that Thai girl in Geylang, I redoubled my efforts. I entered and started to fuck as I usually do. What did I get? More whimpers and protests.

"The mood was rapidly cooling with each attempted stroke, but I was determined to get my money's worth. And I did. Eventually we wrapped it up, though I can't say it was memorable in any positive sense. I left, walked around a bit, and caught a cab back to my hotel. Based on my first time at bat, I have to say Singapore is no Bangkok."

These streets leave you with the ghosts of memory.

Hang a left from Sims Avenue and there you are, Geylang Road, a messy urban sprawl with old pre-war shophouses and eating houses flanking both sides, but, as everyone knows, the real action isn't out there in the great wide open but on the little side streets.

Those little *lorongs* with little short-time hotels, where young women from Thailand can be chosen from plate-glass windows in licensed cathouses and women from mainland China ply their trade more openly on the bare sidewalks; one is legal and the other is not, because open soliciting on the streets is considered a criminal offence in Singapore, but on any given night both sectors of this strange divide rake in the rewards of their endeavours with equal ease for the most deceptively simple of reasons: They can do the selling because someone's always doing the buying.

And so it's hard to even walk down any of those *lorong*s without feeling that nascent vibe so neatly reflected in that old Dire Straits song: "Come up on different streets, they both were streets of shame / Both dirty, both mean, yes, and the dream was just the same." Only in this case Romeo and Juliet get to meet under more capricious circumstances.

Particularly at night, where the atmosphere is almost electric. Charged with subterfuge and stealth. And all because money changes hands.

When you meet her, you might be forgiven for doing a double-take. She's quite beautiful, and she could've been a fashion model or even, if she could've climbed some rungs higher on the sex-work totem pole, an escort or a call girl. But that's never going to happen for the simple reason that she can't speak anything other than her native Isaan dialect. The men who buy her time usually don't speak any kind of Thai at all, except for maybe the ones used to sampling the wares in Patpong or Pattaya, but here in Geylang there is a language that transcends our earthly bounds and actually enables some to escape the bonds of human pain and misery, at least temporarily so. If you have a wallet fat enough to engage her attention, you both have everything you need to keep each other company to fulfil some mutually acceptable level of satisfaction.

And it is this strange dance of desire, if one can rightly call it that, which ultimately offers the single unifying strand that ties up all the loose ends (and, some might add, loose women) represented by Geylang.

There are, for instance, other cities in the region that can offer more things to those insatiable enough to spend money in such a manner. At last count, Indonesia's sex industry generated US$3.3 billion (S$5.7 billion) a year, equivalent to two percent of the country's gross domestic product, and Jakarta even has private sex clubs, where members pay 50 million rupiah (S$10,000) deposits just to join (and several million more just to attend "events") while regular Indonesian sex workers can make 1.5 million rupiah (S$320) a week working out of the local nightclubs. According to a report in the British newspaper the *Guardian,* underage girls (some as young as thirteen and fourteen years old) in Rangoon, Burma, ply their trade for US$100 (S$145) a night; the younger they are, the more they charge.

And Bangkok, of course, has long been famous for its live sex shows, where just a few years ago the girlie bars featuring such exotica were making some 1.3 million baht (S$57,000) a night before the 2 a.m. closing-time curfew kicked in and decimated everyone's profit margins.

Ah, yes, all well and good, but they all don't have what Geylang has: the calm yet calculated semblance of normalcy, of a place just doing business as usual, not gussied up with girls in big hats and badass boots à la Soi Cowboy or pimps in Patpong masquerading as doormen sucking you into strip clubs where you can't pay the exorbitant drink bills and get majorly ripped off, because they think you're too blinded by the surfeit of readily available young flesh.

Geylang doesn't even have the kinky clubs where the girls on one side of the room will play water sports ("golden shower" anyone?) and then let you penetrate them anally, and without a condom if you're willing to pay extra for the sheer dangerous thrill. No, Geylang has always been a bastion of forthright simplicity in a world gone mad with variation. The ever-friendly, ever-indulgent knocking-shop, catering to the whims and fancies of the average red-blooded male who just wants to get his rocks off.

For that, a half-hour romp in one of the regular houses with the Thai girls will set him back a mere S$80, of which the girl herself will keep S$60. An overnight stay is S$120 for the girl and S$40 for the rental of the room, and of the S$180 total, the pimp who rules the roost gets to keep S$40. It's dirt cheap compared to the rates at the KTV bars (where regular sex starts at S$300) and the escort agencies (where the booking fee alone is S$300).

But then you pay for what you get: a room with a mirrored ceiling and even a shower if you're lucky, and a girl who might not say much (because she can't speak any English or even Hokkien to save her life) or even walk right (because she failed at being a model and can't work as anything else).

Out on the streets, China girls will do the same for a cut-rate S$50, with rooms of their own a mere twenty-meter walk away. On some streets further from the main drag you'll also find Vietnamese girls, some charmingly dressed in traditional *ao dais*. And then there are the "independents," who can be likened to the *ronin*, the masterless *samurai* of old, who have no pimps and take their own chances with mercenary zeal.

All so that you can pay her for the convenience that she represents—to please you and then exit your life without you having to tell the mistress or the wife.

And there are the customary, if somewhat cliched, red lanterns actually hanging outside the houses, signifying a working cathouse. Things couldn't appear more obvious, until you spy the Chinese Buddhist (or sometimes Taoist) shrine right next to the lantern. Incense sticks aglow, with the slow burn of the long night to come. The gods will keep you safe from harm in this place, where the company of like-minded ladies will offer shelter from the storm. The sacred and the profane, right here, in one simple package.

And yet there is that juxtaposition of grace and danger that makes it all so enticing. Why, one might wonder, would the United States Navy actually ban its men from even entering Geylang whenever the ships dock at Singapore? (A documented fact, reported in *The Straits Times* as recently as December 23, 2007.) Perhaps it's because Geylang is also a residential neighborhood (unlike Orchard Towers, where military personnel are not at all *verboten*) and also because it would be unseemly to disrupt the placidity of such an outwardly peaceful place. After all, ordinary folks go to Geylang to indulge in Singapore's favorite human activity—eating—and there's a staggering array of, well, everything: meatball noodles, spicy seafood, even boiled frogs served in several ways (though the soup version is apparently good and even healthy).

They also go to Geylang to gamble, even though that's an illegal activity, and police busts are common on the smaller alleys where the gambling houses reside. Police busts also occur from time to time where girls working the streets get rounded up—not the usual vice squad sweeps that you might see in Hollywood movies but rather the usual "let's show 'em who's boss" muscle-flexing on the part of the powers that be to apprehend those overstaying their social visit passes or tourist visas. Prostitution is one thing and actually permissible, but overstaying for even more than one day in Singapore, that will get any plain-honest, hard-working working girl into a whole lot of trouble, and who wants to get deported back to Chiang Mai or Cebu or Hanoi? Now that would really be shameful and sad. (Ask the 680 women who were rounded up during the first three months of 2005 for allegedly "committing vice while in Singapore on social visit passes"—it isn't that you can't do it, just that you can't do it while temporarily visiting for purposes other than actual employment. After all, that's a cash-only business and the taxman needs your money.)

The other thing that Geylang's nightlife offers are the sex shops, all usually clean and well-lit places, several of them located on Geylang Road and offering everything from blow-up dolls with mouths readily agape to all manner of delectably dildo-friendly fare. The quaintest of modern paradoxes surely exists here, since hard-core porn is banned in Singapore so you can't procure the movies of big-name American porn stars like Jesse Capelli, Lexus Locklear, Jenna Jameson, and Tera Patrick (unless you download them online, of course) but you sure can legally buy from here all those synthetically rubberized replicas of their very own private parts ("Savanna Samson's Pussy and Ass" is particularly fetching in its packaging).

So go figure. Is there some context missing here? Are the local authorities being compassionate in implicitly ministering the needs of those sex-crazed dudes horny enough to poke their peckers into things obviously not human? There's no money-back guarantee if the thing's not spongy enough and it doesn't fit.

In the end, it might be laudable that something does exist that apparently subverts the usual one-size-fits-all paradigm so often ascribed to the government-prescribed thinking prevalent in Singapore. After all, the divorce rate is steadily climbing, with more married couples divorcing sooner than usual—divorces and annulments hit a record high of 7,061 in 2006, up from 6,909 in 2005—and six out of ten Singaporeans reported themselves being "bored with their sex lives" (according to the latest Durex Sexual Wellbeing Survey), so somebody must be benefitting from this outlet somehow.

There was also the curious case of the thirty-six-year-old woman from Hunan who openly chastized the men of Singapore in a letter she wrote and personally hand-delivered to the Chinese-language newspaper *Lianhe Wanbao* in October 2007. She had worked the streets of Geylang while on a social visit pass for four months and had decided to literally throw in the towel and was heading back to China, but not before having her final say. She admitted that she charged S$40 to S$50 for sex, exclusive of tips for extra favours, and had worked nightly from 8 p.m. to 7 a.m., with as many as eight men on a good night and two on a bad one, for which she earned anywhere from S$3,000 to S$4,000 a month.

"No matter how well you treat the streetwalkers, you are just a fool in their eyes," she wrote. "When you sympathize with them, you will definitely fork out money to support them. But behind your back they are laughing at how they've conned you.

"I know deep in my heart that being a streetwalker is the lowest of professions. It is what proper people call 'dirty money,'" she added, explaining that she had fallen on hard times back when the factory she owned in Hunan had shut down and her husband was sent to jail for corruption, leaving her to abandon their eleven-year-old son in China to seek her fortune in Singapore. Stories like hers are commonplace in Geylang. There are Burmese hairdressers who have no choice since a hairdresser makes a mere 30,000 kyat (S$6.35) a month back home. A quickie from someone on the street suddenly earns her eight times that in a mere half-hour. Yes, doing the math can get downright scary.

And you can only truly begin to understand when you walk those very same streets, enter those very same houses, discover those very same rooms. There's a pathos to poverty that can make a girl choose the gilded cage, because the alternatives are too horrible to fathom. Here, a good-looking guy in a crisp white shirt and a wedding ring will cozy up to you and caress your thigh, and who cares if he's a policeman? In fact, who cares if he's anything? All he represents is a transaction, and all you represent is a dream.

Her lipstick, mascara, and perfume will haunt you for all time, if she was any good to you at all. That's what you really pay for: a return of sorts on your investment, and you can only hope it lasts.

And these streets leave you with the ghosts of memory.

Jeffrey Kaminsky is proud of being a rampant sex tourist and his two disasters in Singapore haven't dissuaded him. Nor has a hernia operation he underwent after noticing a bump on a certain usually unbumpy part of his anatomy. (It was noteworthy, to be sure, since he actually noticed it during a very wild session with a working girl in Buenos Aires, Argentina.)

"I don't share some people's dislike of the transactional nature of commercial sex," he explains. "For me, I'd rather pay for it and not have to do that elaborate dance and hope I'm getting a good lay. If I'm paying and she's charging, it's a given that she knows what she's doing and has no qualms about doing it. Once again, you have to go with your gut since some are all talk and poor performance. But in my experience, that has been the minority.

"I think the whole idea of brothels is amazing—how they are so accepted in so many parts of the world and how they were so common in Europe up until World War Two, I find that fascinating. I've been to Germany and enjoyed its FKK culture, which continues to flourish, and also Prague, Copenhagen, and Amsterdam. It remains to be seen how the new laws in Amsterdam will affect the sex industry there. They're trying to clamp down on it now, but I think it will probably have the opposite of the intended effect and drive it underground into the hands of organized crime."

What about the necessity for protection and the risk of diseases? "Sure, I hate condoms, but I'd rather use a condom and save my life than have the bareback experience and die. Maybe someday I'll find someone I can do without a condom, but then there's the risk of pregnancy, and the costs to get rid of it. *If* she'll get rid of it. And I'm deeply suspicious of women—who knows what she may try and pull, if for no other reason than to shake you down?"

His antipathy towards women, he admits, stems in part from his divorce—he'd been married some years back "to a she-bitch from hell and we didn't last more than nine months before I decided I wanted out!" From that point on he distrusted all women and decided that paying for sex was going to be the only way he was doing it.

No more roses and relationships for him. This is why he never bothers to splurge on upscale escorts and prefers the lowlife grunge rock of simple, straightforward brothelhood. "Escorts are just not worth the money, in my opinion," he declares. "Fat-cat, expense-account escorts exist everywhere. The businessmen who think they're paying top dollar in Singapore don't know about the Arab sheik/U.S.–Europe nexus, where former *Playboy* Playmates are whisked to Paris for an all-expenses-paid trip to entertain some Arabs, and they don't even have to have sex with them. We're talking petrobucks."

The Vietnamese girl from Orchard Towers was a somewhat different story, of course. Jeffrey was slightly irked that she'd told him she was twenty-five and then admitted, after they got to his hotel, that she was really twenty-eight. "Why she felt a need to be so honest, I don't know," he shrugs. "Maybe she liked me."

Why had he even bothered to ask her age? Egad, had he just been reduced to being a "relater"?

In sex-industry parlance, a "relater" is a john who tries to have some kind of relationship with his girl, someone who attempts, however clumsily, to treat her like a real person. Most hookers hate "relaters"—these guys are a nuisance and a waste of time—unless, of course, they are very rich.

Jeffrey Kaminsky, however, is not very rich. Back home, he was struggling to make his car payments and had spent most of his income from his job as an insurance salesman on the far-flung brothels of the big bad world.

"Well, she told me she'd lied because if she'd told me her real age, I wouldn't have chosen her," he explains. "The truth is, I do like older women. But she did *not* look twenty-eight. Her English was better than I'd expected, though. She said she was from Hanoi, and was willing to come back to my hotel. I prodded her boobs and turned her around to check out her ass. Everything looked good and we started to discuss price. We finally agreed on S$180 for two hours."

It suddenly occurred to him to ask her if she was a ladyboy.

"I don't know why," he recalls, "but I was a little spooked by the whole idea that *she* might be a *he*, but I wouldn't know for certain until we got back to my hotel. She unzipped her pants, took my hand and put it down her front. She wasn't wearing panties and I could feel her pussy. Good enough! I just hoped she hadn't had sexual reassignment surgery. By that point, I realized my paranoia was starting to get the best of me. As we left, I told her I was American and she was Vietnamese and was there a problem? 'Before, yes,' she said, 'but not now.' I tried to ask her a few questions about how she was able to get out of Vietnam and how she came to be a working girl in a quasi-Western place like Singapore without her government questioning her dedication to the communist struggle, but she never really addressed the issue."

He ended the evening by trying to discuss "her dedication to the communist struggle." Wow, had the sex really been that boring?

"I went there, to begin with, because I had already been told about the 'four floors of whores,' a.k.a. Orchard Towers, by a friend," he notes. "He said the building is actually several stories high but the bars are located on the first four floors, hence the expression. So I dropped in during the day, at the beginning of my trip, while strolling down Orchard Road. This was, of course, earlier than when the real action normally began. Even at that early hour, mid-afternoon, the girls were actively shaking down any male who drifted within a few yards of their grip. I was besieged by Filipinas coaxing me to come in and buy them a drink. I had been warned about the bar scam, which is run exclusively by Filipinas. They'll get you inside to buy them one drink, and suddenly you'll end up buying drinks for every girl in the place, and quickly run up a bill of S$100 or more. If you protest, security will explain why you owe the sizeable tab or else. When I told the girls I knew what they were trying to do and how it worked, they relented and admitted it was a shakedown, and quickly lost interest in me.

"I went there again later, at around 10 p.m., and things were definitely in high gear. I saw girls from all over Asia—Vietnam, Laos, China, Indonesia, Thailand—and they were preying on the mainly European sex tourists and expats. Some of the girls were very aggressive. Two Chinese girls attacked me as I entered one bar, promising a threesome, and followed me around until I finally shook them. No sooner had they faded away when another girl caught my attention by grabbing my crotch and tugging on it!"

But why then, despite the initial excitement, had his dangerous liaisons not proved memorable, particularly in Geylang? The problem might well have been something he hadn't anticipated— the general poor quality of clientele these girls had to deal with on a nightly basis. Many of them had revealed in press interviews that the Singaporean men they serviced were usually the worst performers in bed—many of them were clueless about sexual techniques and fumbled around like nervous nellies, making them total killjoys who had cash to burn but less fervor to match. Jeff was battling an invisible adversary—the girls were off-form and off-practice, like athletes lacking sharpness and skill because they hadn't had worthy opposition. Or boxers who were lacking good sparring partners.

"To be honest, I didn't get the impression I was that desirable, except to Filipinas," he now concludes. "I had the feeling I was intruding and that the girls were much more interested in Asian men. I didn't feel uncomfortable, but neither did I feel welcome. I'm speaking specifically of Geylang now. Orchard Towers was another matter entirely—I was way too popular there! But I think my overall feeling of disappointment came from sensing the general atmosphere—that Singapore is all about business—more than any conversations with the girls about the sexual sophistication or lack of among the men. I was also amazed that I never saw any police anywhere the whole time I was there, and I enjoyed that feeling of safety.

"My impression was that sex, like everything else in Singapore, was a business transaction first and foremost, and one to be concluded as quickly and efficiently as possible. That certainly was my experience. Especially the quickly part!"

After a week in Singapore, he jetted north to Thailand, and discovered Hooker Nirvana. "I'm sure the girls are all excellent at their chosen work, but based on my random sampling in Bangkok and Phuket, I have to say Thai girls rank right up there among the best of the best, including the Brazilian girls I had sex with in Rio and the FKK Club girls from Romania. Thai girls are open-minded to a fault, sexually knowledgeable and astoundingly skilled. Frankly, I can't wait to go back. The Thai girl I had in

Singapore was no competition whatsoever.

"Singapore is a fascinating place to visit, but it ranks as one of the worst sex destinations on earth. I tell people now, 'Save your money for Thailand!'"

Mad Dogs and Englishmen

Having a sexual encounter with your own sister isn't something he'd recommend to anyone, since there are long-term consequences.

"Yes, I fooled around with my sister when I was about twelve, and I think in some ways that kind of fucked me up," Mike Sadwick now says. "She was asleep and didn't realize it. To this day, I think she still doesn't know about it. I felt suicidal about it later, when I was at university.

"I mean, with your sister? I think not everybody does that!"

He says it in a voice that mimics Ozzy Osbourne, the famous English rock singer who was arrested in 1989 for allegedly trying to kill his wife Sharon one night while he was severely drunk. ("I mean, for hell's sake, man," Ozzy later told a reporter. "Arrested for murder? That ain't a very good thing.")

Mike says this while nursing his third beer at Tango's in Holland Village, his usual watering hole when he isn't in the mood to quit drinking. He is by profession a television director but by personality a self-confessed chronic alcoholic—he'd been on and off the wagon often enough, perhaps as often as his many visits to Geylang and Orchard Towers. However, to call him a sex addict would be too simple a sobriquet, given his complicated background.

He comes from a pretty well-to-do family, and his father was a clinical psychologist who was surprisingly understanding when Mike confessed his transgression. "I wrote to my dad and explained what had happened, with my sister. I told him that it had made sex a heavy, painful thing for me, and I'd always felt guilty about it. My father actually wrote back and told me not to feel bad about it because 'sexual curiosity among children is very normal.' He said you become sexual around eleven or twelve and I was at that age at the time."

He'd expected some kind of admonishment from his father, but actually received tacit approval! He couldn't get over how crazy that was.

Mike actually came to Singapore direct from his native London, partly because his parents used to live in Singapore and partly because he had "exotic visions" of the place, all of which vanished after he arrived. "I remember thinking River Valley Road must be such an exotic place," he recalls. "I had these mental impressions of a large, flowing river with a lush, green valley, like some glen in the Scottish Highlands but transported to the tropics. Boy, was I wrong about that!"

His childhood roots might well have prepared him for the sojourn. He found himself in Singapore because of his marriage. It's a long story, as they say.

"I was born in 1967," he explains. "My father was a therapist and my mother was a librarian. We lived in Cornwall till I was six years old. I was then transferred to this really rough area in the East End of London—you can still hear the accent when I speak occasionally, if you listen very carefully. Then I was off to Essex to a public school, where basically you didn't live very long if you spoke like that.

"And that's when I started to realize the power of words, and discovered that I wanted to be a screenwriter. You didn't have to be a big guy if you were good with words. That's how I survived the school. I became interested in writing and comedy and into distracting people with laughter. If you can distract them by getting them to laugh at what you say, they're less inclined to punch you in the face." While at university in London, Mike met a Singaporean fellow student and they fell in love and married, and he followed her when she decided to return to Singapore.

The marriage fell apart after three years, because of sex.

"My wife was just not interested in sex," he says, "and I happen to be a very sexual person, so I started drinking to try to lessen my own sex drive. And all that did was make me an alcoholic. I would drink a whole bottle of vodka every night. One night, we sat down and talked and I told her I just couldn't do it anymore and I wanted a divorce."

Once the separation was granted, he took advantage of his new-found freedom with a zeal that, he says now, must have been frightening to anyone else. "I went out to Geylang and basically shagged anything I saw. I just went on a fuck-bender. I mean, really, like in the first six months, every two days. Sometimes, twice in the same day. I would go from whorehouse to whorehouse, even pick up girls from the street. I wanted every single physical type of woman there is, Chinese and Indian and whatever, fat with huge tits or petite and tiny or taller than me, you name it. I made sure I screwed everybody. Now I'm afraid to go down there in case somebody recognizes me!"

"It's sad, very sad," he laughs. "The real fuck-bender part lasted six to eight months. And then after that I started to think, "What the hell am I doing?!! I should be saving my money! Stay home and have a wank, it's cheaper!"

Today, he thinks it "just a little bit odd" that he resorted to paying for sex only after he'd been married, when most men partake of it before they march up the altar. "Literally, I was in bad shape—because there was pretty much no sex in my marriage. My wife was just not very sexual. I'd had girlfriends before, I lived with a girl for six years before that, and that was a very sexual relationship. But apart from that I wasn't very experienced, you know. I never screwed around when I was at university, I was very serious about my studies and I suppose you could say I've now made up for lost time. You stop to consider your mortality once you split up with your wife and I wanted to see what it was like, the experience of being with a woman again, you know. I hadn't experienced that with my wife for years.

"My first prostitute, she was from Thailand, and I was shaking with fear," he remembers. "I had no problem getting it up but I was so nervous. The girl was a woman—she was about ten years older than me. That's how desperate I was for sex and I didn't even realize it! This was about five years ago, when I was thirty-five. I enjoyed it. I enjoyed having sex with her. I was very surprised by her shyness. She was very shy about her stretch marks. But I can't remember her name—their names are the first things you forget as soon as they tell you!"

Well, anonymous sex was what he wanted, and he received it aplenty. "Prostitution is regarded here as a legal activity," he notes, "and the real amazing thing in Asia is that some of the women are really good-looking. They're incredibly hot. Even the older ones have nice bodies, some of them. You never see women like this in real life. And they'll screw you for S$200 or less. At Orchard Towers they'll even give you a discount. For me, that's fine. I'm a very sexual person and I like to have sex for long periods of time, as often as possible. And that probably makes me an impossible pain in the arse for most women, because after three months of dating, they're done with shagging. They want to get on with their lives, whereas I've always got time for a shag."

However, having broken through the doors of perception, what he eventually found on the other side wasn't as liberating as he'd hoped. "People say the great thing about the sex industry is that it fosters temporary relationships which can be quite comforting," he observes, "but to me it's nothing like that. It's about voluntarily putting yourself into a state of delusion. Because the girls are quite good and if they're nice about it, you don't feel so bad about it, especially with the freelancers, the ones who are in the game voluntarily. They don't have long faces and some of them really enjoy having sex as well.

"But I'm not about to go back to Orchard Towers again. I found myself utterly bored with the whole thing. One of my friends back at university, he had this theory that you only get so many girls in your life. He said God only gives you a certain number of fucks. And I think I've used all mine up."

His first date with delusion was with a Shanghai prostitute he met at Orchard Towers. She said her name was Lucy, and she had the most amazing body—as he puts it, "like a sex doll but real, and she was slightly diminutive, just above five foot nothing. She used to say to me, 'When I come to see you, I could have seen six other customers, so don't expect me to give you a bloody discount!' She was funny. I also recall her telling me she had a child, by accident. I did stay in touch with her, mainly because her English was better than any of the others. I could actually talk to her about stuff and have a whole conversation, whereas with most of them, you can't. We kept in touch by email and I told her she would have to leave the sex industry and make a change, because she was going on about how, 'I hate my life, I'm so sad,' that sort of stuff. I knew I couldn't help her.

"I realized then that I'm actually very old-fashioned—I believe in one girlfriend at a time. Or, if it's at all possible, one prostitute at a time. The thing about prostitution is that it allows a man to completely lose his fear of sex and women. You come to accept yourself and you don't have any performance anxieties, you lose your inhibitions in a way. I would never have survived my divorce if I hadn't screwed all those prostitutes. Because having more sex improved my sexual performance. I started screwing hookers because you know you don't love them, that you can't love them. But I will say one thing about prostitution—it's actually more honest than dating people, fucking them and dumping them. It's more ethical, because it's a straightforward transaction."

This is a view many men have when they try to explain why they pay for sex. "When you date someone, there's a tremendous amount of bullshit you have to go through," Mike says. "You have to go out for meals, and you have watch each other eat. I mean, Jesus, it's like watching someone take a shit, you know? It's a dance. And I hate that dance. It's a lie. And I thought, yeah, prostitution, that's the answer 'cos it's honest. But you see, that's my problem. My head is turned every twenty minutes. Even now I'm looking at the waitress at that restaurant across the road there. Hmm, how old do you think she is?"

He believes that the motivation for most guys needing to pay for sex depends on the guy; he isn't comfortable generalizing. For himself, though, it makes sense that he makes his living directing television commercials, since the *auteur* theory certainly fits him like a glove. Who knows, he could even make a movie about himself someday. "For me, I know it was because I never screwed around much before and it was like consolation, being with these girls, which was better than having a wife or a girlfriend. There are people who would say I was deeply immoral, but I was really devastated when my marriage ended even though I was the one running away. I had been faithful to my wife the whole time. We just stopped having sex and that was the only reason we got divorced. I was very frustrated and felt very unloved. Every time we had sex it was a disaster and she would apologize and I would feel bad for her.

"The way it all ended was, one night I got up at three in the morning and went into my editing suite instead of the lavatory and pissed all over thousands of dollars worth of editing. I was urinating in my sleep! I woke up half way through and she was shaking me, saying, 'What the fuck are you doing?!!' I was this pissing man! I managed to control myself and finished my piss and went downstairs and I said to her I thought our marriage was over and there was no way it was going to work out."

However, he's quick to add, he never ever saw himself as a "saviour" to the women he paid for, though he knows the phenomenon is all too real. "Yes, the 'saviour' mentality, that's the fantasy some men have. They fall for that and buy houses in the

Philippines. I never believed any of their lies. To think they have feelings for you when they're having sex? They neither empowered or dehumanized me. I don't regard it as being immoral as such, but I do see it as being slightly unethical. I mean, because the only reason these girls are doing it is because their education isn't sufficiently good enough to get them other jobs. And it's partly their fault. One Malaysian girl told me she was in Singapore so she could screw *ang mohs* (white men) like me. She said she got so-much per hour working at a factory in Malaysia, but having sex she could make a hundred and fifty times that with me.

"I think a lot of these girls are actually idle, they're lazy, and frankly if you look at the guys at Orchard Towers—as Lucy, my Shanghai girl, used to say to me, 'They don't last very long, they don't bother you much, and they're usually quite gentlemanly—they're not violent, or they're almost never violent. And once they're finished, they fuck off again. They don't keep you there for ages.'"

Jim is what he wants to be called. Not because he looks like the English singer James Blunt but rather because that's his actual *nom de bordello*. "Jim means 'pussy' in Thai," he explains proudly, "and when I'm in Bangkok, I always make the girls laugh because I say my name is 'Chim Jim' which means 'taste pussy.'

"When a Thai bargirl asks me what my name is, I literally tell her I want to taste her pussy. Isn't that funny?!!" He says

105

this while giggling like a teenage schoolboy who's just discovered dirty magazines.

But Jim knows he's not in Thailand anymore—he's now living in Singapore. And when it comes to the sex industry, the twain somehow doth not always meet. He's a long-time habitué of Orchard Towers but still finds time to zip north and hang out at his old stomping ground, Nana Plaza, which is where he previously spent an alarming amount of time, often five nights a week, right after leaving his office.

He's arguably the most experienced person in Singapore to talk about the differences between the 'chim jim' cultures of the two cities, though often he admits his world view has been tempered by disillusionment. He can't seem to maintain a lasting relationship with a woman who isn't a sex worker, though not for want of trying. "I really think now," he says soberly, "that I'm doomed to be a hooker-fucker."

"I'm at the point now where I'm bored of this crap," he declares. "Because when you get into actual relationships with women, you have to adapt to them and maybe I just don't know how, or I do the wrong things." With hookers, he adds, you don't need the soft skills that most women require of a real companion, and he's tired of "having the same old conversations—you know, when they say, 'Oh, you berry hamsum man, I want to love you long time, love you only one!' You want to just roll your eyes every damn time they say that."

His conflicts stem largely from feelings of manipulation, he says, but it's always a double-edged sword. Who's really manipulating whom? Back when he was growing up in London, he always entertained fantasies of having sex with Asian women, long before he even had the opportunity to live in Asia. Now that he's actually here, he pays them to service him, yet the bloody bloom seems to have gone off the proverbial rose.

It was a lot more exciting, back when he first discovered prostitution, back home in London. "My first experience with a Thai girl was exactly that—she used sex to manipulate me. She was a call girl in London, though she wasn't one in Thailand before she moved to the U.K. They can cost from £150 an hour up to £500 an hour or more, depending, and you can get some very beautiful women. You can get girls in London who are into fetish and S&M, which I only did on the mild side with one Chinese girl. She was just getting into it and had a madam who was teaching her the kinky stuff. She would dress up in her gear for me, but no whipping or spanking. I wasn't ready for that, at that stage, though I liked the dressing-up part. I was friends with her—I did some web design for her site so I used to get some freebies!

"In London, I had a few experiences with call girls. It was okay, it was pretty good, you know, but expensive. And there's a bit more variety since they cater to a lot more different tastes. The girls I saw were not English girls. There was a lot of illegal trade, especially girls from China and Thailand. A number of them will say they come from Malaysia or Singapore but in reality they're actually Thai or Chinese. I also remember some South African and South American girls, especially Brazilian girls—supposedly, there's a huge market for them—and you hear about them in the news, about illegal operations like massage houses and they get busted and all that. But I think they've changed the laws, and brothels are all legalized now, I think. I don't know, I haven't been back there for a while."

Then he got the call to do some web design work for a company in Bangkok, and off he went. He found the beer gardens of Soi 4 and Soi 7 exotic enough, though hanging out with overweight expatriates looking for nubile flesh didn't always float his boat. Then he discovered Nana Plaza, with its astounding assortment of enticing go-go bars and sundry dark places, and he was gone.

"Yeah, I used to go to Nana Plaza five times a week, roughly. Pretty much after work. I worked quite close to Nana. Just off the BTS and you walk another ten minutes. I was introduced to it by a colleague at the first place I worked at in Bangkok. I was going out with a local girl at the time, a normal girl, so I wasn't single at the time. But I was soon after!"

That was four years ago, and the beginning of his sex addiction—if one can rightfully deem it that. He's actually trying to figure out what it was all about, he says, since paying for sex isn't always about sex. A lot of the time it's about convenience and expediency, and even power. Most men get somewhat defensive about this issue. "Look, I didn't go into Nana completely bright-eyed and bushy-tailed and wet behind the ears," Jim recalls. "I knew what it was. I knew it existed before I went to Thailand but it wasn't what I was going there for. It wasn't the motivation for going to Thailand. But it's there and, I found out, it's unavoidable, though I wasn't instantly charmed."

"Well, okay, after a few beers you can get instantly charmed," he laughs. "When I first got to Bangkok, I liked going to this one place, the Beer Garden on Soi 7, because it was independent and didn't have a barfine system, so it wasn't like a go-go bar." The average barfine—the amount a guy has to pay the bar in order to take a girl out of the bar—is 600 baht (S$25).

"There's a range of expats there, mostly Brits and Americans, not a lot of local guys," he continues. "The girls are mostly part-timers, many of them are working during the day. Not many are secretaries, most of them are probably lower than that, and a lot of them aren't well educated. They come from the countryside and move to Bangkok, typically from Isaan up in the north-east of Thailand. Most Western guys you see with a Thai bride or Thai girlfriend, 90 percent of them are Isaan girls. Isaan girls are dark-skinned, usually quite tall, unlike girls from Bangkok or from the south who are more Chinese-looking. I don't have any preferences myself, I don't have any bias towards any particular group. I'm an equal-opportunity lech!

"So yeah, that was the scene, you know. Rough and ready,

easy availability, and young, a lot of them, not underage but in their early twenties. The going rate at the Beer Garden was cheaper than the go-go bars and that was one of its attractions. Sometimes, I'd also hang out on Soi 5, at a place called Gulliver's, which is a normal bar and has the same kind of girls that go into the Beer Garden but tend to be a bit nicer. There's also Soi 33, but I never go there. It's a pretty dull place, not much happening, there are lots of bars but they're not the same as the bars you get in Nana. Those just tend to be fronts for a lot of organized crime. Soi Cowboy is more fun. It's less intense and different from the Patpong area, where many Westerners tend to go. I find it's too insane there and there are too many young girls, I mean real teenagers."

Like many white guys in Bangkok, Jim found himself repeatedly drawn to Nana Plaza because of the sheer abundance and plenitude of night-time nookie. "Nana Plaza itself, yeah, there's a lot of stuff going on there and I liked it, I thought it was pretty cool. I used to go to this one place called Rainbow 4. A lot of nice girls there, a big place with about two hundred go-go dancers. But it's a barfine system so the girls are quite expensive. The last time I went, I took out two girls from there."

Were threesomes his thing? "They can be," he nods. "The first threesome I had was pretty bad, though. One of the girls had been in a car accident. I realized that I hadn't done any quality control before I booked her! She had a lot of scars and she told me about it as well. I think you have certain expectations when you take two girls out, like you have these expectations that you're going to have a wild time together, and it's going to be perfect, blah blah blah. I guess it's a superficial kind of judgement, just because one girl is a bit disfigured. But then, that's part of the reason for getting into that kind of a situation—you expect that the girl will have a good body to start with, because that's what you're paying for. A good body, good sex, and you're done—you pay her and that's the transaction.

"I think for me the main attraction of all this is the fact that there's no emotional attachment. Maybe I'm emotionally shallow. Or maybe the only way I can enjoy sex is when there is no emotional attachment. I've had experiences in the past where sex and emotions get really mixed up and I felt manipulated and confused. For me, this is 'safe sex'—boom!" He snaps his fingers. "It's just interaction that's a transaction."

The one issue that occasionally raises its ugly head is the spectre of shame. "Not many of the people who go to places like the Beer Garden will ever admit they go to Soi Cowboy or Nana Plaza. Most of them will say they usually go for a beer and have a look and see what happens. But in reality, a screw's a screw, you know? So if you go somewhere cheap, that's what you want, really. And often the girls in the go-go bars aren't as enthusiastic as the freelancers—just because they're more expensive doesn't mean they're any better.

"Ultimately, it's all just about objectification. It basically is that. It's one step beyond masturbation. Sometimes it's unrewarding. Sometimes you think you're just getting lazy. Going to Nana Plaza five nights a week, like I did when I was living in Bangkok, it can be an addiction and you can get used to going down there. Go home, get changed, go out! Everything is there—it's all accessible, no questions asked, no moral issues raised." So theoretically then, what's the difference between that and staying home to wank? "You're holding onto somebody else rather than yourself," he replies. "You could say it's about needing company though I don't know if it's really about companionship. Some guys are into that. But either way, it's about having a live warm body with you—a temporary relationship for two hours! And, for me anyway, it's more about getting a certain feeling of power as well, that you are a person worthy of their attention. This is true especially for guys of my age group, in our thirties, where we are treated better than the older guys you see there. Because they're old and fat and probably want to retire there. People like me just want to go there to have fun, and the girls want to have fun with somebody who's younger as well. They can't go clubbing with those old guys!"

Sociologists have made much, however, of the "saviour" mentality inherent in these schemes, whatever the age group (or, more incisively put, age gap!) and Jim laughs when asked to ponder this phenomenon, almost as if his air of nonchalance has suddenly been put to the test. "Some of the girls have tried to do a number on me in Thailand, especially if they have kids and they're single parents and the Thai husband or the Western husband left them and they're left to support their kid so they want to get somebody who's going to be their sugar daddy. That was never on the cards with me. It's all about awareness, isn't it? Awareness of that happening and being a bit alert, being a bit streetwise, I guess. You gain more experience with time and you can see the signals coming earlier and you can put a stop to that. And anyway, in Bangkok there's so much choice that you never get into situations where you get really hooked on one girl. As soon as they start to get their claws into you—I don't want to sound too misogynistic but, you know, that's it—as soon as that happens, they'll squeeze you for everything you've got. Squeeze you dry, basically."

When he moved to Singapore, he found himself a nice condo in the River Valley area, from where the cab ride to Orchard Road was remarkably cheap and cheerful. "Orchard Towers is a different scene from Nana Plaza," he says. "I'm really in the minor league for that target market, since there are guys here in Singapore with ten times my income so they're better targets. I was headhunted to come here but I'm not on an expat package. I do well but I'm not a typical target for an SPG (a local 'sarong party girl.') Whereas in Bangkok, the gap in income is such that anyone on a reasonably good salary is a target. I haven't been to

113

Orchard Towers as much as I have been to Nana, but I have had a handful of experiences from there, a couple of Thai girls and a couple of Vietnamese girls—a couple of times each, I paid S$250 for long-time. That's not bad, you know. You can get a hand job from a tranny at Clarke Quay for S$150 and the short-time rate in Geylang is S$80!

"The difference is that at Orchard Towers, the quality is very high. The girls are more professional and it's much more transaction-based. I think the girls in Nana Plaza are open for more than just doing business. A lot of them are in that game to get out of the game. They're looking to meet some Western guy who could be a husband, basically. That's what all the Isaan girls are doing it for. They're looking for typically an older guy to look after them and their family. It's common knowledge that a lot of these girls come from farming backgrounds and they're from the countryside, and they're doing it to give money to their parents. In many cases, their mothers push them into it. They come from a matriarchal society, and so the girls are trained from young to always get what they want. The girls are taught different kinds of tricks, how to use their looks to get what they want, how to use sex to get what they want. So, I think, their reasons for doing it aren't different from the girls in Orchard Towers. The last girl I was with, a Vietnamese girl, the reason she was doing it was because her mother's having an operation and she needs to pay for the operation. So she keeps coming back to pay for that. The income gap is quite something—they come from very, very poor families."

So where's the rub for him, since it's pretty clear that to these poor girls, all he really happened to be was a typical *farang* who could be taken for a ride? "Yeah, I guess that's true," he observes. "In Nana Plaza, they are incredibly charming and hospitable to you, which makes you feel great, but in reality, all you really are to them is a cash cow. That's pretty common knowledge if you're an expat there. And if you know that, you're forewarned and forearmed. You know how to always treat any advances, towards getting you sucked into some kind of financial arrangement. My own approach is to back off and hang out with other girls, so they will see that and know the number's up. They'll think you've gone with somebody else. It's a buyer's market, there are always new girls coming to these bars, and it is possible to go with a different girl every night."

His personal motto, he likes to say, is "I am bad at being good!" And part of being bad was to make sure he didn't get suckered into any sort of long-term relationship. "I will sometimes go with the same girl for a week or sometimes for just three days, but nothing lasting with any of them. It sounds very bad but they all have a certain shelf life before they start to make their move. I've been invited to weddings and things like that—these girls were trying to drop me a hint, you know!"

He received a rude wake-up call one night from an unexpected source. He'd heard of the Eden Club in Bangkok, but preferred the Beer Garden. The Eden Club was legendary, mainly for a single white line on the floor demarcating the permissible activities of the girls working there—those on one side would only perform normal penetrative sex while those on the other side would do pretty much anything including anal sex and "water sports" (urinating and being urinated on, that sort of lovely stuff)—and you could also get a "two-girl special" for 1,750 baht (S$73) each, the price being inclusive of the room upstairs for a forty-minute romp with both of them. "Me, I was never into doing anything that wild, except for the occasional threesome, and I never went to the Eden Club. I always preferred to hang out at the Beer Garden. And that's where I, ironically, did the kinkiest thing I've ever done."

"Well, it depends on how you define kinky," he mumbles, slightly nervously. "I don't do much beyond straight sex and oral sex, you know. No anal. Except, well, only this once. It happened when I was very drunk and it was with a ladyboy. She was more beautiful than any girl I'd ever met. After I took her to bed and found out what the deal was I thought, well, I'm as drunk as a skunk so what the hell, let's try this and see what it's like, you know? But I couldn't maintain any kind of excitement, if you know what I mean, and the alcohol didn't help at all. It's nothing I would ever want to do again. It didn't do anything for me, and it just wasn't my thing, really."

He shrugs, as if to say, "Well, now you know. I fucked a ladyboy in the arse and I lived to tell the tale!"

Go ahead and judge me, he gloats, see if I care.

Mike Sadwick has heard of Chim Jim, though he hadn't heard about the ladyboy episode.

"My goodness, I don't know if I would ever do that, drunk or not!" he exclaims. "My own thing is I like young girls. Well, everybody prefers young girls, up to a point. Up to the point where you get arrested. That's where you stop!"

He laughs, orders one more beer—well, he had just about given up sex so what was the point of giving up drinking now? —and then discloses his deepest, darkest secret. This one, he concludes, was even worse than shagging a Thai *katoey* in Nana Plaza, at least for him. After his disastrous marriage and Geylang girlfest, he took a shine to a teenage model. "I saw her at a studio where I was shooting and I couldn't keep my eyes off her. She had just turned sixteen, and I was smitten. I went out with her for the next two years.

"And then one night, two years later, after she'd just turned eighteen, she came back very late. We were living together by then. I asked her where she'd been and she said she'd had a late shoot but this photographer had paid her S$500 in cash for the work. It was for his own portfolio, basically, not a professional job for a catalog or magazine, so she'd accepted because the instant gratification of getting that kind of quick cash was just too good to turn down. The guy had had some kind of sick fetish too—he'd tied her up with bondage rope and watched her pretend to struggle. That was how he got his kicks.

"Don't ask me why, but I got a bit suspicious when she told me that, and I did some checking up on the photographer, and I found out he was this fifty-two-year-old American who liked to think he could be Helmut Newton someday or something, and he had a reputation for, shall we say, extracurricular activities with his 'portfolio' models. So I confronted her with it and she broke down and confessed that yes, the S$500 wasn't just for posing without her clothes. She had given him a blowjob too, right at the end."

Mike lost it. "I told her, 'Look, I don't need a girlfriend who's a hooker. If I want a hooker, I can go out and pay for one!' We had big old row about that, lasted all night, and we didn't talk to one another for most of the next few days. That was the start of the break-up, because what that did was make me think of revenge. I went back to Orchard Towers and picked up a pretty young Laotian girl and fucked her bunny brains out."

He knew, though, that his own number was up when he found himself trying to explain the great film directors to one of his Orchard Towers girls, a Cambodian lass who was all too happy to make S$250 listening to this inebriated English wanker prattle on about how great Fassbinder was. She didn't know her

Rainer Fassbinder from her Ingmar Bergman, of course, and was drinking single-malt Scotch with Mike, who was definitely too drunk to fuck. Which suited her fine.

Mike says he'd read *Among the Thugs*, Bill Buford's brilliant non-fiction book about the phenomenon of English football hooligans, and he once discussed it at length with a fellow Englishman, a commodities trader named Gordon. The English, as the theory goes, are an essentially angry people. And blokes like Mike and Gordon and Chim Jim, all products of the uptight English public school system, were automatically perfect candidates for hooker-fuckerhood. *Mad Dogs and Englishmen*, to quote the famous Joe Cocker album title.

"Seriously, what is the thrill of having sex with hookers all about? I tell you what it is, mate," Gordon once told him. He had moved to Singapore from Hong Kong, and at one point he had two Thai working girls living with him in his Cairnhill flat and was part-time pimping them. "There are guys who like to think all prostitutes really love it, and there are definitely ones that do—you can tell from how wet their nether regions are, you know—but I've slept with some girls who were like sandpaper, d'you know what I mean? So uninteresting. I stopped because I got bored. What really did it was my mate Bob is an alcoholic who always tries to get shagged without having to pay for it. And he got into a very big fight with those two Thai girls one night at our house, and the police came and all that, and it was a big mess.

I also remember waking up one morning at some hotel in Geylang and all my money was gone, my wallet was gone. What I found was that it was all so soulless and I got to the point where I felt slightly disgusted with myself. I mean, it's like, at what stage do you stop?"

Mike also recalls Gordon's favorite Asian hooker story, which has such a heartwarming ending. "My first experience with a prostitute was when I was nineteen years old," he'd recounted to Mike. "I was flying to Australia at the time via Manila, because Philippine Airlines was cheap, and so I fly into Manila and the bloody plane breaks down. We get told there won't be another flight till the next day. So I'm hanging out at the bar drinking and I meet these Australian guys who've been on a two-week shagging holiday and they ask me if I want to go to a girlie bar. I'm like, 'Fuckin' hell!' and go. I'm nineteen and it's a new experience, you know.

"So we get to this go-go bar, full of the obligatory fat Germans sitting there at the bar with these girls dressed in bikinis. And when you're nineteen you get a fucking boner just like that, you know. This girl started rubbing against me, telling me I'm so handsome. She's just too sweet, and so I take her back and she's nineteen, so we went all fucking night—shagging and coming then starting all over again. The next day, I walk down to breakfast with her and everyone's staring at me for being so audacious, and the waiters are all looking shifty. It was a really opulent hotel, marble columns and all that. I tell them to be nice to her. She's a little village girl and she never goes to these kinds of places, you know, certainly doesn't go down to breakfast in the morning like that, so I wanted her treated with respect. I enjoyed her company. But after that, I got to Sydney and I got the fucking clap! Got a really bad case, like pissing into a fucking tree!

"So what I'm saying is, these guys come out here and they want to have a good time, but these girls are like sharks and you're the fucking blood. They move in on that, they make you feel great, and the next thing you know they're moving in with you! So do I think these guys think they want to rescue them? Yeah, if they're naïve and they've never been through it. They all want a whore in the bedroom and a lady in the kitchen. I think it all comes down to how much sex you had when you were younger. I got laid left, right, and center back in England. I'd have three or four girls at the same time. So my ego didn't need bolstering when I came out here. I don't mean to sound arrogant. So when three of these girls start hanging on to me, it doesn't make me feel better, it actually makes me feel worse. Like, what am I doing here? When I could be out meeting a normal girl and getting laid that way. The thing I hate most is pretentiousness. There are guys who say they never regret anything. Oh really? I fucking regret a lot, you know.

"And the other thing I hate is misogyny—men who hate women—and I think that goes a whole lot deeper than most people think. Like there are men who use prostitutes because when they were young, all their mates were getting birds and maybe girls would laugh at them because they weren't as good-looking, so maybe they end up treating women the way women used to treat them. Sometimes, I think it is about that."

"But," he told Mike, and Mike never forgot it, "they don't realize it's not just about sex." Which is why Mike looks upon his experiences with bittersweet forlorn. Having sex with prostitutes can be nice until you actually get personally involved with one, but damned if you do and damned if you don't. If you make it a habit like Chim Jim, you can find yourself feeling empty and hollow, the "hooker-fucker" who can't sustain a "real" woman's interest and has to resort to monetary transactions for feminine company.

And if you find out your own girlfriend's been selling herself on the side and behind your back, you can't contain the irony enough to expunge anger at your own sense of betrayal. Mike was trying to capture a butterfly who, by nature, needed her freedom.

"That's what I've learned the hard way," Mike now says, somewhat wistfully. "You can't marry the temple harlot."

Filipina Fiesta

How can one man's life be so profoundly changed by a single, seemingly innocuous building in Singapore?

To understand the world view of Dave Robinson, though, one needs to see it through his eyes. Bespectacled and bookish-looking, he could be mistaken for a college professor, except for the way his pupils will spontaneously dilate whenever he's within earshot of that one particular building located off East Coast Road.

Old habits die hard, it seems, in light of how his relationship with that building has cost him dearly with one relationship after another hitting the rocks and finally gave him a new lease on life when he met the girl of his dreams. The last two women happened to be working at bars in that building—known to the general public as Paramount Shopping Centre.

Could it have been worse? Sure, there could have been more women thrown into the mix, not that he doesn't fraternize with enough already. The common denominator is that they all happen to be Filipina.

That's what happens to it at night. By day, Paramount Shopping Centre happens to be a typical air-conditioned consumer hub, so common to this ultra-clean city-state aiming to uplift itself from Third Worldhood. Basically, it's the mall that sits next to the Paramount Hotel ("Your ideal getaway with a tradition of impeccable hospitality," as the hotel's brochure proudly declares. "Walking distance to idyllic beaches. Near mega-malls, shopping centres and various food-centres, famous local eateries and restaurants . . . Once you've tasted the allure of this part of our island paradise, you'll always want to make Paramount your home away from home!") But by night, the ground floor of bars and pubs is gleefully transformed, some say, into dens on iniquity, watering holes suitable only for those of ill repute.

In some of the other bars, the girls will strip semi-naked and dance with customers or, more brazenly, undress to the booming hip-hop beat and boogie down for everyone to ogle, right on top of the bar counter. Singapore's openness to bar-top dancing, as was the fashion in recent years, had on many a night certainly been given brand new meaning.

"Well, hmm, how *did* I discover it?" Dave replies when asked. "I think I must have walked by and saw it. I do remember that I rounded up two friends, an English guy who worked in the oil industry and this Italian friend, and we went there one night, and we had a good time. This was quite some years ago, probably around 1999. At that time, there were only a handful of bars in there, nowhere near what there is now. Now, I believe there are 23 of them. Well, it's 23 if you count one of them that got busted by the cops and suddenly got 'closed for renovation.' I was told an undercover cop saw someone getting a blowjob under the table."

"At the time, there were only six or seven, maybe eight bars open. It was a bit more open back then, not the kind of lurking around that you get nowadays, if you know what I mean, with the girls in the corners doing whatever they're doing. It all changed for a very simple reason—it just got commercial. One of the girls that owned the first bar we went to was a former bargirl herself, and she ran this bar which got busted for girls giving blowjobs—they called it 'indecency in public' or something like that—and the owner went to jail for a couple of years. This was in 2002 or 2003. They closed it down but the guy got out of jail and reopened, but with other places and using other people's names. This guy apparently owns four or five pubs under other people's names as well, elsewhere in Singapore. Anyway, he reopened that notorious bar that I mentioned, the one being 'renovated,' under somebody else's name."

The real action never takes place in the Paramount Hotel, though you can bring a girl up there if you can pay the regular room rate of S$158 a night. The bars are all located in the adjacent shopping mall, easily accessible through a glass door at the far end of the hotel lobby. The relatively innocent, generally more tame bars are on the side closer to East Coast Road and the more notorious ones are on the other end—it all gets crazier and crazier the further one walks towards the front of the hotel, which faces Marine Parade Road. The bars have names like Club Fire and Crescendo, and they resemble those in Bangkok's famous Soi Cowboy but without chrome poles and go-go dancers.

Interestingly, the men's toilet upstairs—on the floor above, where there are only regular shops closed for the evening (and no bars at all)—charges 30 cents per entry, while the one downstairs (where the bars are) will let men in for free. Did the bars work like a cartel, absorbing the costs of the toilet entrance fees, for the sake of good business?

Dave went to Paramount one night with his friend Mike Sadwick, an expatriated Englishman, and they walked into a bar called Fortress. It was Wednesday, a slow night. A group of Filipina girls chirped and cooed, and headed straight for both of them.

Mike, being younger and blonder, was mobbed much faster than Dave, and he immediately fled outside. "My goodness," he yelped. "One of them grabbed my testicles!"

"These girls," Dave tells Mike, "are the last of the great romantics."

They are clearly there to make a living but, he insists, they're looking for love. And, he declares quite openly, so was he. He certainly wasn't getting much love from his marriage.

He'd found himself a favorite girl in one of the bars, but she got busted by the cops for overstaying her work permit and was, after a traumatic period of detention, deported back to Manila. Distraught over his culpability in the whole mess, Dave bought her a house in the Philippines. This, despite the fact that she was apparently very possessive; Dave is not allowed into the bar she used to work in. Meaning, in Filipina-bargirl parlance, if he is even seen setting his sodden foot in there, one of her girlfriends will report back to her by cellphone text messaging and, to put it politely, he's dead meat.

Ah, yes indeed, the last of the great romantics.

He laughs mockingly, with more self-deprecation than one might think for someone in his position. He says he has spent a lot of time thinking about why he is so attracted to these girls.

"I guess I like Filipinas because culturally they are Asian but they're very Westernized, and they've got this Spanish thing and this Catholic thing," he muses. "I'm not Catholic myself but I find that attractive, and I like their darker skin as well, so I really like their look. I find them interesting because culturally they are very gentle and respectful, though that's not to say they are submissive—that's not true at all!" Most of the women at Paramount, he believes, "would rather do something else rather than work there. In fact, I think, they'd do anything else other than that, if they could."

As veteran journalist Sheridan Prasso points out in her fascinating book *The Asian Mystique: Dragon Ladies, Geisha Girls and Our Fantasies of the Exotic Orient*, published in 2005, adult literacy in the Philippines is at 95 percent, one of the highest in Asia, but there are girls who never finish high school and are thus "at nearly the lowest rung of status in the Philippines, virtually unemployable in any profession requiring any skill." These are the girls one sees at Paramount, and in the bars and brothels across Southeast Asia, because they are driven not by choice but necessity.

There is a barfine system back in Manila, just like in Bangkok, and it costs a male customer 1000 pesos (US$18)—the bar's fee, which he has to pay before taking a girl to a hotel room. The bar pays the girl half of that (500 pesos or US$9) and the bikini dancers in go-go bars all cost the same for this transaction.

"Why they all hang out at Paramount is something I don't quite know," Dave says. "I guess it just sort of built up—there used to be a minority of Malay girls and in a few bars you could find Malay girls and even Indian-Singaporean girls, but they all seem to have been shipped off. Now, you can't compete with the numbers there. The Filipinas probably congregate together because of language, I would think.

"The girls there are usually Catholic, and this means they have a way of rationalizing what they do. Uniformly, if you pester them, they will tell you they do not like what they do. They will all say they're doing it just for a while, and yet they come to work every day looking like they enjoy it—'I'm doing this to support my kids, I'm not doing anything wrong, tomorrow's a new day,' that kind of thing. And that part of it, I think, there is a Catholic thing about it that fascinates me. That's something that is very, very different from the Thai girls at Orchard Towers." There is a mystique to these girls, which he enjoys and participates in, akin to being in a co-dependent relationship with a drug addict or substance abuser.

Sheridan Prasso, in her book, notes "the gap between outward appearances and the reality. After all, cultural norms in the Philippines, including Catholicism, were imposed by Spanish colonialists. Clearly they did not wipe out attitudes towards sexuality, they just drove them under the surface." She also cites a 1982 study called "Sex and the Single Filipina" which concluded that, on the surface, young Filipinas appeared sexually conservative, having been raised in Catholic households, yet "nearly 80 percent had experienced cunnilingus and fellatio before age twenty-one, 94 percent had experienced manual genital stimulation by boyfriends; 72 percent had had premarital intercourse by the age of twenty-one."

The same study also noted that in 1967, "psychotherapists detected more regret among women who were virgins at marriage for not having experienced premarital coitus than among women who did experience it," and that "85 percent felt no anxiety, guilt or feelings of 'loss' of their virginity the first time they had sex. The only anxieties among the remaining 15 percent had to do with what might happen if their fathers found out." Prasso added that when she studied the same thing in Japan, she discovered that women in a non-Christian culture may not feel "guilt" in terms of "sin" but they do experience "a negative feeling from violation of societal values" and so "this Philippine study seemed to prove that Catholicism's strictures weren't the only factors in creating sexual mores. Filipina girls raised in strict Catholic homes had all kinds of sexual experiences as teenagers, and did not feel guilty about them."

Dave agrees with these findings, and says his Filipina fetish grew out of his own attraction towards Asian women. "I've never really liked Caucasian women. I've always had a thing for Asian women, even back when I was in Australia. There was only one Chinese girl in my high school and I dated her, and that says something. I grew up in a little backwater outside Melbourne, a place called Morwell. According to town legend, Morwell is derived from the Aboriginal term 'more willie' meaning 'woolly possum.' It was a very weird place that wasn't very outwardly looking. I guess, because of that, I was always culturally curious and even at a young age my world view was fairly broad.

"That one Chinese girl in high school was a start, and then I dated several Caucasian women and it wasn't until university that I dated a half-Korean woman, and that's when I got the 'yellow fever'—or the Asian fetish, whatever you want to call it."

Often, Dave can be seen at one particular club, more laid-back than the others, an easy-going *karaoke* bar where people actually take turns singing. There is always, in such places, one "permanent" girl (the *de facto* "employee" with the actual work permit; every bar is required to have one) and in this particular bar he is particularly good friends with the girl, who tends to emcee the proceedings by hogging the microphone and passing it to prospective warblers.

She herself actually sings quite well, and Dave often does a duet with her, with one microphone each. Their favorite tune happens to be that Foreigner classic, the one everyone knows, so aptly entitled "I Want to Know What Love Is." (It could be everyone's theme song, of course, given the context.) Dave also remembers when one of the girls at a Paramount bar called Brizo started stalking him. She sent him a bunch of text messages the very same night, right after they'd first met. He'd made the fatal error of buying her a drink and did she take a shine to him. It was in October 2007 and the first one arrived inside his cellphone at 12.57 a.m.

"Hello! Hw r u? R u still awake? sorry f m dsturbing ur sleep . . . thank u 4 d drinks, thanks 4 chosing as ur partner. . . I am well, free, dnt think am expensive. I am nt, 8s all up 2 u, m nt dmanding . . . i really hd a bg reason why i do dis, 4 my daughtr education"

Dave knew the scam, because he'd been through this before. "Okay, my interpretation is this," he says. "She's happy because I liked her enough to buy her a drink, and she hopes for some form of relationship—meaning usually 'girlfriend'—which would mean I would help her out, you know, like give her money to top-up her phone card or buy her regular drinks or lunches or gifts, possibly even actual cash. By 'don't think I am expensive,' she means not sex for money but she'd be happy with any help I can give, even just visiting her and buying her drinks. But, certainly if she achieves 'girlfriend' status, sex will follow shortly. Partly, they know it helps to keep you close. But these Filippinas are also damn horny—It's that Catholic thing!"

A few days later, after he'd intentionally failed to reply to her text message, she sent him another one, logged in his phone at 8.26 pm:

"Mahal can you help me? I need to boke a ticket early because the plane ticket is too very expensive. 360$ that I don't have, my salary is not enough. Mahal!"

Perhaps the most telling of her messages was one he received a week later, after he had once more declined to reply. This one was sent, amazingly, at the ungodly hour of 9.28 am, when most of the girls would usually be fast asleep. Oh boy. Perhaps she'd taken the night off, for a change, and was up bright and early, in a sanguine mood. It read:

> *One of the biggest forms of flattery is knowing*
> *that by just being your normal, wonderful self*
> *you make someone extremely insecure! . . .*
> *YEAH!u g'mOwnin*

That seemed very desperate to him, and not funny at all.

She didn't even bother to spell "Good morning" correctly. It was a complete turn-off. He ignored it and hasn't heard from her since. But that didn't mean life would return to normal.

There he was, looking like a fool to most of the outside world, having actually given money to buy a house in the Philippines for a Paramount bargirl who had been barred from re-entering Singapore, and he was still sending her money despite, as he admits, not having seen the girl for almost a year. She'd already been replaced and he was now in love with someone new, another Filipina who had started out working first in Hong Kong before landing at Paramount.

Some would surely call him yet another white male expat in Asia infected with a common illness—the need to "save" these silly girls.

"I agree that yes, maybe the 'saviour' thing is part of our male DNA," he admits, "and there is some of that in me. But I don't think that's what's been guiding me in terms of making the house payments. I think that was more about the personal relationship and the life that I'd had with her. I totally admit I still love the woman, even though she's back home in Davao now and I haven't seen her in over a year. I made a serious commitment, that we were going to be together forever. I still care for her and I still love her, for sure.

"So yes, I'm screwing around, and I'm going to leave her high and dry, and so the least I can do is help her financially. It's about me living up to my commitment, at least part-way, since I did say we were going to be together and that I was going to provide for her. I didn't think I would do that for anybody but for her, I felt it was the least I can do. This isn't some casual relationship with a bargirl. After she got deported for her visa problem, I went to visit her and she was quite traumatized by the whole experience. So we agreed that we were back on, and she had bought a house, a small one with the money that she had been making. She had two kids so they needed a roof put over their heads, so I said, 'Okay, since we've agreed we're going to be together, I will help you financially."

The place itself lies outside Manila, he explains, where it used to be farmland but the government had now created subdivisions for new housing. "Manila itself is too crowded now," he grumbles. But why had he truncated the relationship *after* agreeing to buy the house? "Because of the separation—the distance, it's very hard on me. This other girl came along and I definitely fell in love with her. She's a very special woman."

After that girl got deported, Dave consciously avoided Paramount for the next year and a half. "I stopped going there, because I was just so angry about what had happened to her. Anyway, one night, I was coming back from a work function and had been a bit drunk and I thought I would just stop by and see what was happening—I couldn't resist—so I went in. And I suddenly felt like, "What the fuck am I doing back here?!!!" I ended up talking to this one girl who had just come back from Malaysia and she had gotten raped in Malaysia by her agent, her Filipino agent. He had withheld her passport and locked her in the bathroom and raped her.

"And I was, like, 'Uh, okay, I gotta go!' It was, like, boy do I regret coming here!" But of course before he could make it out of the building he met someone else who, a short time later, became his girlfriend.

Well, his detractors would probably say, he might have met her anyway at some other bar somewhere else. And also, if he hadn't started helping the first girl financially, somebody else would've come along and done the same. These girls live by their wits, after all, and lesser men have in the past fallen for such feminine guile.

"Well, that's possible," he shrugs. "She told me she had a Chinese boyfriend here and they were going to get married. He was from a typical Singaporean family so the mother hated her because she was Filipina and looked down on her and all this shit, so she was kind of trying to back out of that. She told me she had to, because life with him was going to be hell. I don't know. If I hadn't come along, I'm not sure whether she would have married him—she could have married him just for the security, though I don't think so, knowing her."

But how well did he know her, really? Meeting these girls at bars where you have to yell over the loud music, how did that facilitate intimate revelations?

The way it tends to work, Dave replies, is for the guy to get the girl's phone number from her after chatting her up at the bar, and then call up to offer to take her out to lunch. "Since lunch is a form of transactional payment, right? You could argue that," Dave notes. "You never outright pay for sex right there at the bar. Out of all the ones I've known there, I've only ever had sex with three of them. Three might seem like a small number but that wasn't what I was after and not what I was seeking. I think the people who go there for something else are deluding themselves, because that's not what they're going to get there."

"But that delusion works well, right?" he laughs. "I do go to Orchard Towers too, once in a while and I have done take-away, more than once. There's a Thai girl who's supposed to be getting back to town today, in fact, and she said she was going to call me. The thing is, they don't speak English very well so, yeah, sex is all you want. The sex is not as good as what I have with my current girlfriend but it does fill a need, basically, even though that sounds a bit harsh, depending on how you define prostitution.

"I will say, mate, that if you do become a 'customer' then you will see them let their guard down and you get to see them as they really are. They do find ways to hit you up for money and the phone top-up thing is quite a common move. You really get to see the whole range of it with these girls. The thing you have to remember is that there is a really wide cross-section of these girls. They're not all stalkers. A lot of them are really nice and they are respectful of who they take money from."

He recently got into a big fight with one of his friends, a drinking buddy, who said: "Why do you go to Paramount? These girls are all prostitutes!" They haven't spoken since.

"I think there is a fundamental misunderstanding about the place by a lot of people," Dave insists. "The place is not about that. It's about a business. Most of the girls there, 90 percent of them, do not do that. Sure, there is maybe ten percent, but an absolute minority, that will. But the vast majority of them, no way.

"Yes, you do hear all this stuff about the blowjobs under the table and the naked girls dancing on top of the bar counters. But that's good for business, that's the way to bring people in. The whole idea is to trick people into thinking they're getting something when they're not. At the end of the night, you might be grabbing her arse but you will probably never see her again after that. She's just there to get you to buy her drinks and nothing more is going to happen beyond that. Even for me, I wouldn't say it was all about me trying to find a relationship with someone there. It was never about that. That happened out of me going there."

To explain the sheer complexity of his perspective, and perhaps also illustrate his ongoing fascination with the girls who work there, he tells his favorite Paramount story. "I was driving home one night and there happened to be a vice raid. Two girls came running out and they were freaking out. So I said: 'Get in the car!' I gave them a ride. They had just arrived in Singapore, and one of them could hardly speak any English. She was a very *kampong* girl, her English was barely there, she was very dark-skinned and had worked out in the fields.

"So we exchanged phone numbers and I would go see her a few times. We went to the parks a few times and had a little fun in the car, nothing serious. I used to go visit her where she worked, and her favorite trick was to get on my leg and kind of rub herself back and forth on my leg. It was an amazing experience. She would gaze up into my eyes—she would wear this iridescent eyeshadow, and there was this fluorescence reflecting off the iridescence—and she would have this *grin* on her face as she rubbed herself back and forth on my leg—rubbing her crotch, basically, meaning she was masturbating herself on my leg.

"She was wearing something underneath, though, and this is the point. Once I found out she was wearing real panties and I was surprised, because they all usually wear g-strings at the club. I asked her about this and she said, 'Oh no, I was on the bus and I am shy so I am wearing two pairs of panties.' The total irony of it! Here's a girl who is too shy to sit on a bus with her g-string on and then she comes to the pub to rub her crotch on your leg. This sums up the whole thing! When these girls go into the pub, they switch into a different mode. If you see her on the street the next day, she would probably be so shy, she would probably not even hold my hand. I think that encapsulates the whole thing— she wears two pairs of panties on the bus because she's shy but at work, she's a whole different animal."

He got serious with his current girlfriend after that, however, and so the leg-rubbing ended. The girls have a not-so-secret language, he then learned, like a private semaphore they deploy when staking out their turf. "What they do is, she will walk with me to the toilet and she will hold my hand walking through the center part of the bar, so that all the girls will see, like, 'He is mine. Don't fuck with me!' At one time, I had three concurrent girlfriends going—they were all working in different bars and it gets tricky when you decide to visit them. I made sure I went the right way so I wouldn't be seen by the others. They are *very* jealous. Even with this one that I'm in love with at the moment, I'm very careful whenever I'm at Paramount and she's not. The Filipina Mafia, they are bloody strong—if I run into the wrong person, she'll get a text message within five minutes and she will know I'm there!"

The strangest thing about Dave, one could say, is his almost touchy-feely sense of admiration for the girls, and he is always quick to defend their honor. Particularly when it comes to their commercial instincts, however flawed the backstory.

"I know of one girl who had been a paralegal," he recalls, "and she made more money working at Paramount than she did as a paralegal back in the Philiippines. She told me she needed help because she felt bad about the work she was doing, so I was touched by that and tried to help her get a job with a friend's company.

"The first girl I fell for made about S$60,000 to S$70,000 in that one year she worked there. That's a lot of money to them. With that, she can send her kid to an international school or buy a plot of land. But now she has no money and it's her birthday this weekend and I just sent her S$100 so she could buy beer for the party! A lot of these girls spend money as fast as they get it. That's the cliche that you hear. A lot of them are like that. But I also know those who use their money to buy houses and buy land. The level-headed ones are not foolish at all. They'll buy themselves a nice phone but they'll also make smart moves by buying houses. My current partner is a good money-earner. I know it sounds strange that I would be able to find love at the Paramount. Stephen Leather's book *Private Dancer*, that's the norm. Most people would say all you would find there is heartbreak."

So what's going to happen when his Davao bird discovers that Dave might have helped her out by sending money but isn't going much further?

"Nothing," he replies. "I mean, she'll be devastated. She doesn't know, but she will find out about this new girl, for sure. The first one, her generation is gone, they're all in their 30s now and they're too old already. Most of the girls at Paramount are about 25. The youngest girl I have ever met there was 19, but that's quite rare. A lot of them are 26 or 28 because a lot of them have kids. They all have husbands who have left. It's a Filipino male pasttime. They get the girl knocked up and they bugger off to find somebody younger, better-looking, whatever."

She sips his beer and shrugs. Maybe that's why these girls are working there and looking for love. And maybe that's why guys like him go there, to see if he can snag one of these lovebirds and whisk them off into the proverbial sunset—in the guise of looking for love too, at least on the outset. Dave says he's actually quite proud of being a time-honored denizen of Paramount and he's happy to share his knowledge of such a unique place. "Once, I was at that notorious bar, the one that got closed down for 'renovation' after the vice raid. I went with two friends from Hong Kong, two *angmoh* guys who had been living there for a long time. They were giving it to me about how boring Singapore is. And then I took them there. At four in the morning, they were getting their faces smothered by their girls who were squatting over them, And they said Singapore sure wasn't boring anymore!"

On his frequent business travels, Dave always explores what other cities have to offer by way of their ladies of the night. And he always returns to Paramount.

Perhaps he had been in Singapore too long and had gotten used to being so conveniently serviced. The laissez faire nature of the commercial sex trade elsewhere somewhat unnerved him. "Wherever I go, I always try to find the underbelly. I did that in the Middle East recently. There was even a bar there in the basement of my hotel, and sure enough 80 percent of the girls there were Russians and Ukrainians and surprisingly about 20 percent West African. Well, one of them was from East Africa. I met the hottest girl I've seen in my life. She was from Djibouti.

"And I would have taken her home with me but she would not go lower than US$300. I could not believe that! I laughed when she said that, and she just walked away. And I just went, 'Wow!' I don't know whether that rate was short-time or long-time—we didn't even get to discuss that! I just thought she was joking and she just walked off!"

In Thailand, he prefers the go-go bars over the normal bars. "I guess I just prefer the go-go format, which is more straightforward while the others are more about pretense. I can see why someone would say the opposite, though. But you know, even in Bangkok it's all spread out and you have Soi Cowboy which is more laid-back and a local expat hangout, which is what Nana used to be. All the expats went to Patpong and all the locals went to Nana, and then the Internet came and Nana got blasted all over the Internet and all the tourists started going to Nana and destroyed the place. Now you have the Russians controlling all of Patpong and Pattaya."

Singapore, by comparison, was much more innocent. What one usually saw was what one got, usually free of distateful, organized-crime elements. Dave likes the fact that places like Paramount existed for those like him, men who enjoy squeezing Filipina flesh the same way that others frequent, say, the Malay KTV bars. The girls are there to blatantly service the male hormonal urge for interracial sex. "I remember reading about the Malay girls at the KTV bars and I thought that was really cool. I mean, there are actually these places in Singapore, places where I have never been!"

His friends tease him about being a Filipina sugar daddy. Word had gotten out fast about his sending money to the Philippines. "I'll admit, the 'sugar daddy' thing is a real phenomemon," he observes. "I can have a relationship without forking out money."

Now, if anyone asks him what might be the wildest thing he's ever done at a Paramount bar, he'll just laugh without saying much. "I've had my fingers in lots of interesting places," is all he'll usually offer.

He'd rather not discuss the details of his future plans. But he intends to continue helping his first girlfriend financially. "I did have a serious conversation with my new girlfriend about moving to Australia. But no, I see myself living in the Philippines. I like the place. My aim is to move there eventually and semi-retire, run some kind of business or something. It's a great place to retire. I can't go back to Australia to retire. I keep going lower and lower in the economic scale. I keep having to find someplace cheaper. Lower cost-centered!"

He laughs, perhaps at the unintended irony. He had certainly chosen correctly and was getting, pardon the pun, the most bang for his buck. Falling in love with someone while he was trying to get the hell out of there? Now, that was sheer serendipity. He might never, ever be that lucky again.

PART THREE

Last of the Independents

Big Bad Mamasan

The rooms are just dark enough, conferring an eerie intimacy more akin to an occult reading or a seance, though channeling the spirits is certainly part of the plan.

Some hard liquor, followed by some carnal arousal, those kinds of spiritual activities. Aided and abetted by an older lady usually referred to as a *mamasan*.

Such is the netherworld of the Singapore KTV bars, where *karaoke* is just an excuse to book a private room for things much more interesting than singing. "Yes," Mamasan Nicole says, "number 109 is very pretty but she has a bad attitude. I'd take number 116 if I were you. Lily is tall and slim, she's from Nanjing and doesn't speak much English. But she's a very good singer. The girls are not allowed to do any kind of nonsense in the rooms. We always prefer if the gentlemen book them to go out, back to their hotel rooms or wherever. If the price is negotiated and the girl is *willing*, then the deal is done."

At age forty-two, Nicole looks half her age, not an unusual thing for most Singaporean Chinese women, and her wavy brown hair bears the distinct results of much perming, coloring, and rebonding, all necessary in an industry where image is absolutely everything. When she's not all dolled up herself in the best possible manner, she's exhorting her girls to comport themselves better for the constant inspection of the men at her establishment. After all, she herself grew up in Hougang, and her Taoism-oriented, conservative Chinese upbringing instilled in her some virtues relating to presentation. She likes being neat and tidy, and expects no less from her girls.

"Sometimes the girls here, they will wear the same dress again and again, because they think they are with different customers all the time," she grimaces. "Or they say things to me like, 'Oh, I always wear this because I have good luck, all the men like this.' I ask them if they even bother to wash their clothes! I say to them, 'Today, he may see you in this dress and think you're very pretty. Tomorrow, he'll see you in the same dress and think you're very dirty.' You will be surprised. I have had customers ask me, 'Hey, that girl, does she ever change her dress?' Men do ask me this sort of thing and I think, oh gosh. Sometimes I just wonder.

"Sometimes I do get tired of this. I do get sick of this line of work, in the sense that you can have problems with the customers and they don't understand what you're facing. The management has a certain set of rules they have to follow and the customers will tell me, 'Why should I follow these rules? I'm paying the money!' So sometimes, because I'm the middle person, I'll get scolded by the customer and things like that. Sometimes, it can be unfair."

Then there are downsides to the job, she adds, like all the health issues. "I will say this frankly—as a *mamasan* I can tell you—we do not promote these activities but the girls will sometimes have sex with the customers and I am always telling them, 'Whenever a customer books you out, please make sure you have a condom with you.' They are not niave. You cannot work here and still be niave, but some of these girls are real idiots. For a few dollars they will save the money—can you imagine? They will ask the customers to buy the condoms. And some customers are nasty, they will say things like, 'I don't buy. I don't use, can or not?' And they will pay more to have the girl not use a condom.

"Most girls will not go, frankly. Most of them would not *dare* to go. Because for the few hundred bucks that you earn, you could get a disease. And then what happens? Most of the girls here, I would say, are smart enough not to do that. We don't provide condoms here—that's their own business—we don't do that because we are not pimps here. We just tell them to take precautions, that if you want to earn money, you have to learn to take care of yourself."

Nicole sounds mildly agitated whenever this topic comes up. Like all *mamasans,* she doesn't earn a basic salary. The work is entirely commission-based, so she only makes whatever she can get from liquor sales and the booking hours of her girls. The whole idea is to move volume, to get those girls going with the guys as much as possible so that she herself makes more. Watching her eyeing her girls lounging around in the club's main bar area isn't all that different, in some ways, from the way a farmer might view his sheep milling around inside a paddock.

They're quite fascinating to behold, these girls from mainland China. Some are dressed in revealing outfits, exposing enough skin to test the limits of public decency. They sip their drinks and chat among themselves, all fully knowing that they're there to be appraised like slabs of meat on a butcher's block. The wealthy men come and go, drinking them in with their eyes, seeing them as merely their consumer choices for yet another evening's entertainment.

It's already an open secret as to what actually transpires here, she notes, especially with most of the girls being foreigners, lending an extra layer of taboo to the whole tableaux. "A few years ago, I had just one fair-skinned Indian girl here—Singaporeans don't work much in the clubs over here," she discloses. "The majority of the girls come from China or Vietnam. The percentage of Singaporean and Malaysian girls here is really very small. Why? Because the China girls are more daring, in the sense that they are willing to do anything for customers. I would say that sometimes you have to take your hat off to them. They really really have the survival instinct. They are willing to do *anything*, which sometimes I think is not so good if you have customers who are a bit more prim and proper, like the businessmen who are entertaining clients over here.

"When I say 'willing to do anything,' I mean going back to

the hotels with the customers and sometimes even doing kinky stuff in the rooms. Stuff like that, which is actually not allowed in this club. Our club is a proper nightclub so when we have girls doing nonsense in the club with customers, the staff will inform the management and we have to do the dirty work—tell them they're not supposed to do this or do that. We will tell the girl to lay off, because we might lose our license. You never know, there may be anti-vice officers walking around in plain clothes. Everyone knows what can happen in the rooms but it's a matter of, 'Don't be caught!' We try to prevent that if we can. Sometimes, even for us as *mamasans*, we tell our customers that if they want to do a lot of nonsense with the girls, they must go back to their hotel or book her back to their hotel room. At least there you can do whatever you want. This club does not allow girls to do short-time in the rooms. Not even a blowjob. If you want to do that, you have to take her out of the club if she's agreeable and go to a hotel, because for us the main thing is not losing our license." The authorities enforce a demerit point scheme to keep things in order, and points are docked with each police bust which usually means earlier closing times.

The income earned, in actuality, varies from month to month and club to club, but the outlay numbers alone indicate a great deal. Here at Nicole's club, a basic room costs S$150 and a bottle of Chivas Regal S$228. There are more down-market places elsewhere that will charge S$90 a room and throw in a free bottle of vodka during happy hour, and regular-hour prices are S$138 for a bottle of Chivas Regal, though you can also fork out S$144 for a bottle of Martell if you're feeling rich.

If you're not feeling so rich, Johnnie Walker Black Label is S$128 and, for the real cheapskates, two jugs of Heineken beer are S$38 nett. But who comes here to drink beer? That is usually sold at clubs featuring skanky Filipina girls who might be part-time maids, not this club where Nicole and her girls find themselves in the upper echelons. There are some really fancy rooms here, where the men can slouch on extra-large couches and even shoot pool, rooms big enough to throw full-scale bachelor parties. Inside all the rooms there are always at least three television monitors facing the main couch. One of them is permanently stuck on the sports channel—some of the guys who frequent this place are big on sports betting, particularly on English Premier League football—while one is the actual *karaoke* screen where some Japanese, Korean, or Mandarin tune warbles along (with equally sappy boy-meets-girl visuals, because, well, one has to maintain a modicum of innocence).

The last screen is the one that actually matters. In some of the small rooms, all a customer will see on that third screen is a sequence of still photos of pretty girls, each captioned with her club number for easy selection. In the larger rooms, this third screen is a much more sophisticated thing of shock-and-awe splendor. Little square boxes repeatedly blink with changing numbers. ("R8

BILL" means that the guys in room 8 are leaving and are calling for the bill and the girls have to go to the room to collect their tips.) Because this club operates on a "butterfly" system, where the girls can flit freely among the rooms, each girl's number will show up on the screen when she's wanted. ("R8 101" means girl number 101 is being requested for by someone in room 8.) The whole club seems to run like clockwork, almost as if an unseen hand, an omnipotent force, is somehow guiding the proceedings.

Of course, not all transactions occur only on the premises. Nicole has about a hundred girls under her tutelage, and of these as many a twenty can be placed on call—for special customers who can book them without actually setting foot inside the club. This secret segment of her China girl crew is what nobody openly talks about, since it's the equivalent of actually having escorts at work right here in the club. This is precisely why some escort agency owners have complained of competition from the KTV clubs ("C'mon," one of them said. "Everybody knows, KTV girl S$300 can screw, what? I heard the really pretty ones can go for S$2,000.")

Nicole looks bemused whenever she gets asked about it. "I have never thought of the escort agencies as competition to us. Because what you're asking from us is not the social escort type. You could estimate that for every one escort, there are probably ten KTV girls. That's probably true. But you're talking about these hostesses. I find that the girls who work in the social escort business are usually better looking, in the sense that they are better groomed, more professional, more eloquent. They speak well, whereas the girls here, you're talking about China girls. What do you get out of them?!! Some of them, sometimes, their makeup is so thick! Some of them are too stubborn and think they're beautiful in every way. I have told some of my girls they don't dress well and they look awful. I always tell any girl, 'If you want to work here, you have to take care of your figure, your hairstyle, your complexion, and the way you dress. Because the first thing a customer sees is your appearance.' We do teach them, but some of them don't want to listen."

She laughs, aware of the self-deprecation. "That's the price difference. I'll be very frank. If the customers want to pay for quality, they will still go to the social escort business. They may not have as many girls as I do here, but they have quality girls." And, she adds, the economies of scale are somewhat different, as is the entire business model. "I know how the girls in the escort business are being paid at least S$100 an hour, if you want to generalize and talk about average numbers, and I would think that's pretty expensive."

However, at any one time she has more girls at her beck and call than any one escort agency has girls to readily dispense on the fly, and there are just more business big cheeses with fat-cat expense accounts who will indulge in whimsical, profligate spending. The overnight rate is about half that of what an escort would make, but the turnover of girls is much more rapid on any given night. The open-plan nature of the clubs, with the large bar areas where the girls freely mingle whenever they're not busy in the rooms, also enables far greater freedom of choice for the randy businessman on an after-office prowl.

"The only thing is, I would say, at the escort agencies you know the girls inside-out, and you never have to worry about the girls stealing from the customers," Nicole observes. "But with these China girls? No way will I not worry! There have been incidents where my customers have had their wallets stolen and money taken, and sometimes there are cases when a customer has paid them to go back with them to their hotels and at the last minute they say they cannot go and refuse to pay back the money and leave. 'My boyfriend is waiting downstairs for me at the hotel,' that kind of nonsense. So that's the thing—if you pay for an escort, it may be costly but you know it's safe."

That kind of hard-nosed reality check is exactly what one might expect from Nicole, who's seen it all, having been a KTV *mamasan* for a whole ten years now. Her beginnings were highly unusual for a *mamasan*, in that she never ever actually worked as a 'KTV girl'—she was never a hostess herself—and actually got her start working in hotel management. Then she answered a newspaper ad and went to one of the KTV places, and scored a job there as an assistant manager. She learned about this business from a behind-the-scenes perspective, from socializing with the club members. It's actually the perfect training ground for any aspiring *mamasan*.

"I think what I am doing now isn't all that different," she says, "except that this is a nightclub and not a disco or a hotel. They paid me pretty well there and it was all so new to me back then. I was a bit green at that time, but I soon got the idea what was happening. I'm basically doing guest relations like they do in the hotels, since my primary contact and main source of income is from the guests themselves. I've been at this club for four years now, and I think I'll stay for a while. I'm only forty-four and there's maybe ten years more to go, I think."

She likes this club because of the classy ambience, the core group of girls and customers she has accrued over the years, and the "butterfly" system. "Other big clubs have their own class of customers and we have our own," she muses. "In the sense that during the night, those clubs are strictly booking joints. Booking girls by the hour. It's more expensive. Over here you pay for the 'butterfly' system, where the girls move from room to room. What you pay at those other big clubs, for the same amount of money that you spend you can sit with a couple of girls. They can see a variety of girls, because the girls go from one room to the next. Some people like it better here in the sense that people are moving. It's a lot more interesting here.

"Firstly, the men get a variety of girls to see. Secondly, it's cheaper. And, thirdly, with people constantly moving around in the club there is an energy, you know. If you sit in a club all night with nobody walking around, it becomes very boring. Even now, if you ask me to go back to my previous club, I wouldn't. I did go back there once and I thought it was so boring. It's totally different. They do an hourly system over there and the energy is just not there. Somehow, the trend is changing these days, more towards the butterfly system. But there are a handful of customers who would rather just go straight to the room and book the girls."

So what's it really like for her, as a woman, to see her girls selling themselves to the highest bidder? "There have been quite a few, let me tell you. I had this customer, he's really rich, but he was drunk one night and he stripped and took off all his clothes, right there in the room. I had to go back to the room and tell him to put his clothes back on. I hate to see naked men in the rooms and he was fully naked. I had no qualms telling him to get dressed. He was dancing in the room, fully naked. I told him he should go to a strip club to dance. The girls were in the room and some of them were screaming and some of them were laughing.

"I mean, what have we not seen before, you know what I mean? It's a very ugly sight. You would not expect that of a businessman who is so rich and so well known outside, that when he drinks a lot he becomes like that. The next time I saw him, I didn't mention it. It's not nice to embarrass him. I suppose he's even forgotten about it by now. I mean, we're all adults, and naked is naked, but there are certain things I have to settle on my own. I think that if a man had told him to put his clothes back on, he might have become violent and started a fight because a man dared to tell him to put on his clothes. But because I was a woman, he probably thought, 'Oh, well, maybe I should do as she says.' We do have some customers who do drink and get violent, they start scolding the staff and the girls, and all I have to do is smile at them. When you smile at a person, he can't do anything, he will feel very stupid by shouting at you."

That's her hotel management background at work again, which proves nothing is ever wasted as you walk up your personal yellow brick road. "One thing I've learned is, it all depends on how you talk to your customer and how you handle your customer," she insists. "If he is violent and you are soft with him, he will not do anything to retaliate. We had an incident here one night with a violent customer. The *mamasan* was scolding him and shouting vulgarities at him. He took an ashtray and whacked her on the head!"

There were also cases of drunken Japanese guys lifting skirts blatantly and groping the girls in plain sight. "Yes, and you can't say anything, because the customer is enjoying himself. If you tell them, 'You can't do that!' he will probably say, 'Well, why should I come to your club then?' I mean, as long as he doesn't completely strip her in the club and do nonsense, just pulling her skirt up is, for him, just fun. But I will also say that there are customers who do take advantage of the situation here. Some of them, the moment they get here they will start touching the girls and putting their hands all over the girls, and even for me as a *mamasan* I think it's pretty disgusting. I mean, you haven't even spoken to the girl or asked her what her name is, you don't even know who the hell she is, and you're all over her! And then fifteen minutes later, he will say to me, 'This girl is not fun, she won't allow me to touch her, get her out!' And he doesn't even pay her a tip or a token. That is not right. I mean, if you do that in public, you'll be sued for molesting her and get put in prison, you know. How can you not even have the courtesy to pay her a tip and then ask her to get lost? I said to him, 'You want to try another girl and start molesting again?'"

This floating world can be such an illusion and a trap, and Nicole often has to counsel the unhappy girls. "Every girl who works here does so because she needs to make a living," she declares compassionately. "If given a choice, I would not want to work as a *mamasan* either. I would rather work as something else. But I was thrown into this line accidentally and, frankly, a lot of *mamasans* here, they do not have good marriages. They are either separated or they are divorcées, and some of them are single parents with no husbands. I am separated from my husband myself, for three years now. It's like, the money here, I would say, is pretty good. At least we can take care of our kids. We can save some money and things like that. It's just that the hours are a bit late and working in an environment where there are men every night, we see too many things in life. That's how I would put it. Also, you can't outright tell your friends, 'Hey, I'm working as a *mamasan*!' They will look at you, you know, and go, 'Oh?!!' People from the outside, from the office world, they will not think this is a decent line of work. They will go, 'Oh, she's a *mamasan*, she must be the easy type, every night she's in the company of men.'"

The long nights take their toll, too. "If I do happy hour, I start at 6.30 p.m. and I can finish at 3.30 a.m. or 4 a.m. But sometimes if my customers leave early or if I have no customers for the night, I can finish by about midnight or 1 a.m. Sometimes on weekends, like Saturdays or Sundays when we do not have any customers, we will not come in. You can get tired, from drinking and all this. On public holidays, I'll come in unless I don't have customers coming in. If I don't have any customers coming in, I will stay at home and rest. But otherwise, this job is seven nights a week."

Some clubs are also changing their system of parceling out the goods. "We can have our own girls, but most nightclubs these days have the girls under the company, no more under the *mamasan*. Not all *mamasans* have girls in the nightclubs. Some *mamasans* even have zero. These are the *mamasans* who will take our girls to sit at their tables and do all kinds of nonsense. When I have customers and I need to find my own girls, I can't find them. I get very frustrated with this, and I think it's not fair. If you want to work here, you should have your own pool of girls. If you don't have girls, don't work here. Don't take my rice bowl.

"Now what's happened is the company finds the girls and takes care of the girls and they're all under the company, so if I need a girl I just go to the company. That's why you see they're all waiting outside, in the main bar area." She heaves a sigh. Many weighty issues rest nightly on her shoulders. What a weird job she once had, making men happy by sending her not-so-innocent lambs to inevitable slaughter. The new system doesn't entirely absolve her of responsibility, though. It merely shifts the blame.

"Now I just go out there and pick them," she says. "I don't have to waste time recruiting girls."

Male Order

Some guys have all the luck. That's what Jason says his friends usually think, at least the few who know how he used to make his money. There were some special ladies in his life.

Over a two-year period, in fact, there were ten of them—well, ten that he can actually remember. Of which four returned to avail themselves of his services. "It doesn't sound like many," Jason shrugs, "but I had fun."

Fun? He has done what some men would probably give both nuts for (although that's an unrealistic sacrifice, given the importance of them nuts in this particular scheme of things). Jason, thirty-two, brown hair and blue eyes, who now works as a commercial photographer, had been that paragon of virility so prized by women in the know: a male escort.

And not your garden-variety gay male escort, as some might initially think. He was a true-blue, straight-arrow heterosexual rent boy. True, it was moonlighting, a side job that was almost a hobby, but he was always paid directly, and in cash, by those ten women.

"Some of my friends think I look gay," he laughs, "but from my track record I can assure you I'm not. In fact, I can remember the exact number of women I've slept with. At last count it was sixty-five." That's a reasonably nice number for any sexually active Caucasian male living in Asia, particularly those like Jason with a penchant for Asian women. For those two years, 2003 and 2004, he played the traditional courtesan in role reversal, the infamous gigolo of many a legend and lore. Call him what you will, but when he expires from this mortal coil, he would like to be called (pardon the pun) a lucky stiff.

"You want the short version of a long story?!!" he chortles as he surveys the familiar landscape across the Singapore River, perched appropriately at the alfresco bar outside Hooters in Clarke Quay. A Thai waitress wearing the Hooters uniform— the bright orange shorts and white tank top emblazoned with the words "DELIGHTFULLY TACKY"—waltzes by with his beer. Her name tag says she's "Dahlyn" and this spurs Jason to spontaneously wink at her. She smiles back demurely but quickly turns away.

"Dahlyn? Darling? What a cool name," he murmurs, but she doesn't hear him, having scurried beyond his grasp. "What's wrong with these women here? Don't they know how to flirt?" He smiles as if to say it's no big deal. Women, to him, they all just come and go.

"Okay, here it goes," he begins. "I'm originally from New York. I arrived in Singapore in 2003. I had been in Japan for five years and fell in love with Asian women there. So when I moved from Japan to Hawaii and then to here, I felt like I was in paradise!

"I had heard about escort work from a friend of mine. I had been hanging out with him at the bars on Boat Quay. He said, 'Hey, you're a good-looking guy who probably doesn't have any problems finding women. But why don't you try to make some money from it?' I looked at him and I said, 'How do I do that?' And he said, 'Become an escort.' He said it wasn't difficult and he had some contacts for me. And I said, 'Okay!' And that's how it started."

Like any kind of sexual situation, you always remember the first time. Jason (not his real name, of course) was introduced by that friend to a woman from Shanghai. "He set me up one weekend to meet her," he remembers. "She was a beautiful-looking Chinese woman in her mid-forties and she was here in Singapore for a couple of days. She came to Singapore on a monthly basis. She told me that a lot of the time it wouldn't involve sex. I would be accompanying her and going shopping with her, or going with her to special events. So I thought, 'Okay, what the hell, I'll see what this is all about and give it a shot.'

"So on her next trip, she called me up and said she had a couple of business dinners to go to so why don't I go with her. I said, 'Sure, why not?' So I went out with her one Friday evening and it was to an event and then afterwards for drinks. She paid me S$500 cash. I stayed with her for about five to six hours.

"And I remember thinking to myself, 'Wow, this is too easy!'"

The next day, she urged him to go shopping with her. There were two hours of that, and then that night they slept together for the very first time. She paid him another S$500.

"I found out that she was married with two kids back in China," he recalls, "and she had found out that her husband had a mistress. He was always away from home, supposedly on business, and so she said, 'Well, if he can do that, so can I!' She was quite neglected. And she was wild in bed! I was quite surprised. She told me she hadn't had sex for a while. She was very easy to be with and a lot of fun. When I think back now, she was one of the best clients I had."

It snowballed from there—she introduced him to some of her girlfriends, and he received additional clients from the same friend who had set him up in the first place. Most of the time he was paid his going rate of S$500. He did once get paid S$1,000 "for going out to dinner and shopping and then, of course, sex. Overnight, which means till the next morning, when I would have to leave the hotel."

"It's always hotels," he notes. "I've slept on some nice sheets." There are two in the Orchard Road area that he particularly likes and he has spent many an evening there, suitably lodged in post-coital slumber. The S$500 jobs often involved spending the night too, but he would usually leave not long after sex, as opposed to actually snoozing in the loving arms of his female procurer. Most of the women are "thirty-plus and in the middle- to upper-income brackets. These women have no problems with money."

But such pleasure often has perimeters, and so there were limits he had to observe. He never flew overseas with any of them nor did he ever go to any of their homes. "It was always in hotels. And I've never been paid by a local woman—I mean, there were no Singaporean women. They've always been Japanese, Chinese or Indonesian. I think it's because I live here and they also live here, so this is not the place to play. I've asked a few Singaporean women, actually. I mean, I've asked them if they would like my company and be willing to pay for my time. And they *all* said no."

Amazingly, when he was escorting, he only ever kept one cellphone number—the very same one the ten women always called him on; he never used a separate line for his regular social life. And during that two-year period, he actually dated several other women simultaneously, while he was being used as an escort by the foreign Asian women. "I was still doing this on the side, because it was money. It was quick cash. And of course, being a man it was easy for me to separate the emotional from the physical. It's different for women.

"I mean, I was with quite a few of them who were married but they were at the point where they weren't getting anything more out of their marriages or they were in abusive relationships, so

171

they needed an outlet. I was very happy to be the outlet. I mean, I love sex, you know, and to get paid for it, that's even better!"

The gig did come with its occasional kinks, so to speak. "I had one woman who wanted to tie me up. And I said no. I don't know why. She did ask if I minded her tying me up and I said that, as a matter of fact, I did mind! I just wasn't into the whole bondage/domination thing. I told her so and she was cool with that. But I did get a few strange requests. And they were always from the Japanese.

"Three or four Japanese women I was with wanted to pee on me. I would just lie down in the bathtub and they would hover over me and pee over my dick. I didn't have to drink any of it or that kind of stuff. I was just lying there, not wanking or anything, though, of course, I was turned on. The thrill for them was to just pee on me, and for me it was a turn-on."

Did they pay him extra to endure the golden shower? "No. They didn't pay extra for that. I just thought it was funny. In the beginning, I thought it was weird. But it was quite a turn-on, and one time it almost made me come when it happened. She was just sitting right over me and I was hard. I didn't penetrate her, though I almost did.

"I did also have one woman who was having her period and, as we were changing positions, I pulled out and noticed I was all covered in blood. She was having her period and didn't know it was coming! She was very embarrassed. And, for me, it was an instant turn-off when I saw that. She got all apologetic and wanted to know if I still wanted to continue. And I said okay. I just had to block that out of my mind. We didn't even bother to change the sheets—we just put towels over the bed! This was in a hotel. I can't imagine the look on the chambermaid's face the next morning!"

Despite the usual, somewhat cliched reasons for his "yellow fever"—like many Caucasian men in Asia, he finds the local women attractive for their apparent "softness" and supposed feminine charms—he says he has also met those who aimed to tease rather than please. He recalls one occasion when he hit on a rather fetching waitress at this same Hooters in Clarke Quay. She flirted back and told him to wait an hour, and she would then leave with him when her shift ended. He ended up nursing his beers for two hours, only to finally discover that she'd already gone home.

Another time, another girl offered to have sex with him but then told him she was "just joking" when he agreed to take her up on it. The mating dance in the "real world," he declares, can be a real pain so escorting is actually preferable. Because both parties operate within the confines of a mutually agreeable, prescribed sphere. There is a safety net, and no mistaken missives or hidden agendas. Full disclosure, followed by full disrobing.

"It is also different sexually with these women," he adds. "I find myself getting even more turned on when I know I'm being paid for it. It's also because they're random women, you know, they're total strangers. There is a certain thrill to having sex with a total stranger. I mean, I find myself getting turned on and ready to go just thinking about it!"

For a man to pay for sex, he says, it's about asserting control but when women pay for it, it's about establishing a connection. "I think that I was there to fill that need, to help them, because they wanted companionship for a while. For me, really, to be someone's boy toy for a while, that's erotic, that's a turn-on for me, because it's so outside the boundaries of normal behavior. I come from a typical Catholic family and I grew up in a very strict family so I didn't have much fun when I was in middle school and high school in New York. I could never go out and stay out late at night and I didn't really have the opportunity to have a girlfriend. It wasn't until after I graduated high school that I discovered sex. I lost my virginity to a Japanese girl when I was in Japan. I slept only with Japanese women in Japan. Then, in Hawaii, I was with five of them.

"But one thing about Japanese women I've discovered, which is something I didn't like about them, is that they're not into shaving or waxing. They're always very, very hairy. When they have their legs spread, you can't see anything! I'm very particular about that with a woman. I like them clean-shaven. A little bit of hair is fine but,"—he pauses—"I think maybe, culturally, they have a thing about it. At least so in the late nineties, since that happened for me around 1998."

His favorite sex position is doggy-style, preferably done outdoors. "I like it because I can see myself going in and out, and I've got her ass to hang on to," he enthuses, his eyes glistening feverishly. "I love being on top as well, because I can look at her and I can kiss her. The visual thing is very important to me. I also like doing '69' and I like 'spoon' even though it's lazy sex."

His escort gig clearly allowed him to perfect his sexual repertoire. But, in the end, did he feel like an expert?

No, he laughs, more like a sex therapist. He often found himself being both father confessor and surrogate lover. "I have had occasions when I was with some of these women and they would ask me how I know so much about how to please a woman. When I used to tell them it isn't rocket science, they would just look at me and then they would usually say they had been with many men before me who really were clueless. They really didn't know how to use their cocks or even their fingers. I hear that all the time!"

He learned about sex in an unusual way—when he was fifteen, he bought himself a sex doll, made of rubber. "I was a teenager, you know, what can I say? I got rid of it after a year," he recalls. "I haven't used one again since then. Now if my girlfriend's not in the mood, I just use my hand." He laughs and says the rubber doll was an innocent, juvenile obsession. He'd procured it by mail-order and remembers being so excited after it arrived that he had a whopping orgasm with it just after a few minutes. "I had never been in a relationship with a real woman at the time, because I was shy and, being a virgin, I often fantasized about what it would be like to have sex. I found the doll through an ad in the back of a porn magazine and I thought I could use it to gain some experience.

"I needed to feel confident. I paid US$60 for it and it took a good ten minutes for me to blow it up. I think it was a huge turn-on for me at the time, because of the novelty, because I could imagine it was a real woman I wanted to have sex with. The thing about a sex doll is that once you have it, you can have it forever, provided you don't destroy it by using it too much! Guys who pay for escorts, I think they like to do that for the variety. But it's quite an expensive thing to keep on doing and I didn't have that kind of money back then."

In due time, though, he graduated to playing with flesh that was real, as opposed to merely realistic, and over the years gained the confidence he'd been looking for. "I lost my virginity a few years after using that sex doll. I remember my then-girlfriend telling me that she couldn't tell that it was my first time. Until then, I had never told anyone about the sex doll—I thought it would be kind of embarrassing if they ever found out how I got my first sexual 'experience.' Now I don't mind telling people. I have learned since then that nothing, no sex doll, can ever really replace a real woman."

He sips his beer again, and then divulges his trade secret. "For me, I'll always get the woman to come before I do. I pay special attention to that and make sure to take my time. They hate it when a guy does a ten-minute romp and then falls asleep. And I believe in kissing her all over her body and not just between her legs. Women often have several erogenous zones. Sometimes it's the nipples or the thighs, or wherever. It's not hard to figure out what a woman likes."

However, did he ever feel like a mere convenience to be used and then discarded, like the way many men often treat female prostitutes? "No, at least not with the women I have been with," he replies after a sober pause. "I saw them a few times so we did have a connection of some sort. Even with the women I've had sex with casually in real life, as opposed to my escort life, my percentage of 'regulars' was a good 80 percent. But I will say this: with the women who paid for my services, the number I actually kept was none. I never saw them again because they're from elsewhere. The money thing was kind of a bonus for me, something when I needed extra money.

"The way it worked was, I never kept in touch with them after the dinner, or beyond the job. If they wanted to see me the next time they were in town, they would call me up. A lot of the times I didn't even keep the numbers because they would call me from their hotels and those were the only numbers I had. I would meet them, and that was that."

Lately, he admits, he's been thinking of escorting again. "I know if I do it again, it will be for the same reason, for the quick cash. Also, with my current girlfriend, I've been with her a while, so it's sex with the same person, you know. I think we men just like variety. I did the escorting thing in 2003 and then into 2004, and in 2005 I got into a serious relationship and so I got away from that scene. I deleted all their numbers, the ones still stored in my cellphone, because I felt all that was in my past, you know. My current girlfriend is Malaysian Chinese. She doesn't know about any of this. And I will never tell her. I don't think she would understand."

"I did try calling the escort agencies last year, when I was thinking of getting back into it again," he adds. "Most of them were very rude to me. Was it because I'm a guy and because I'm Caucasian? I don't know. When I told them that, they immediately said, 'I'm sorry, we're not hiring,' and hung up. I got that so many times. One guy did call me back, and he said he had a bunch of expat women and they were looking for a male stripper, and it was S$250 for twenty minutes. I told them sorry but I don't do strip shows. I don't feel comfortable doing that."

What if the gender roles were reversed, if say he had a girlfriend who was an escort? Would he find that at all palatable? "I really don't know how I would feel about that, if I found out that my girlfriend worked in this business. If I found out from the word go, if right from the start she told me that's what she did for a living, maybe I could accept it. But I've never encountered that. It's a very good question."

He then discloses that he recently "sort of went back" to his old life after meeting a cute nineteen-year-old college student, who was interested in photography. "She asked if I could teach her photography," he recounts. "So one day, we went out to Sungei Buloh, which is a wetlands reserve near Kranji. And after half an hour or so of talking about photography, she came right out and told me she wanted to have sex with me. And we did it, right there in Sungei Buloh, in different areas, all around. She had a tongue stud and I told her I had never made out with a woman with a tongue stud before. She gave me the best blowjob ever!

"She then wanted to have full-on sex but she was having her period. My girlfriend doesn't like giving blowjobs but this girl, she told me she *loved* giving blowjobs! She knew I was in a relationship and I asked her if that bothered her and she said no. She sent me a text message the other day, when I was out with my girlfriend, and she wrote: 'I want to fuck you so bad! Let's do it!'"

He laughs again, sporting an aw-shucks grimace. Like, dude, it's such a tragic position to be in, you know. Can he help it if he's such a babe magnet?

Looking like the cat that ate the canary, he then concludes his Sungei Buloh saga. "Well, what happened was I added S$25 to her photography fee. I told her that typically I would do it for free but I did teach her an hour of photography so I said could she 'do something, for the sex part?' She said, 'Sure, how much do you want?' And I said, 'Twenty-five bucks?' and she said, 'Okay!'"

It was finally happening—he was being duly compensated for his sexual services again. And by a girl, after *she* gave *him* a blowjob! (Shouldn't he be paying her instead?) It was his initial foray back into those chartered waters after a three-year hiatus.

"It *was* like going back to getting paid for it again," he grins. "She had a nice little body and I didn't think twice about it. But I've seen her again since then and found out that she's had twenty-five different partners and she is still very sexually active with some of them. So now I really don't know about having full-on sex with her. It might not be the safest thing for me to do."

"When I first met her, though, it never even occurred to me to think, like, 'Okay, here is an opportunity for me to cheat.' I just blocked that out of my mind." He'd been bristling about losing those old phone numbers, regretting he'd deleted them when he did. Now he knows that his svelte young "photography student" was just a forerunner, a sure sign of things to come.

After all, he admits, he's a sex addict. Getting his fix again was always just a matter of time.

Bondage Girl

"How did I come to realize that I'm a very sexual person? Well, let me tell you!" She laughs. "When I was ten years old, I wanted to be three things: an artist, a writer, and a prostitute."

"And that," she emphasizes, not merely for effect, "was when I was ten. Even as a kid I would masturbate, like, five times a day. It's my life. My sexuality is my life. After I broke up with my last boyfriend, I felt really super-free, like I can just go fuck anyone now. I don't always do it, but it's good to know I can just check someone out and fantasize about the possibilities."

At five feet two, delicately petite even for a Singapore Chinese girl, she's small-boned enough to look like the wind might blow her away. But she's discovered that Caucasian men in Asia just love her type, and she knows how to milk them for money.

The look is just her calling card, and she knows it's just a game.

She calls herself Alexandra, after the Leonard Cohen song, "Alexandra Leaving," which, she says, is truly the theme song of her life. Its poetry rang true for her, with lines that recall Keats or Shelley or any of the doomed romantics, about feelings she had harbored over the years; about so much that went unspoken, or was inadequately expressed.

And you who were bewildered by a meaning
Whose code was broken, crucifix uncrossed
Say goodbye to Alexandra leaving
Then say goodbye to Alexandra lost.

The last thing that had happened to her in a big way was her final, angry spat with her boyfriend. He'd confronted her one night after she'd come home late. He'd found S$500 in her purse that hadn't been there before and wanted to know how she'd got it. And there, in his comfortable apartment on Robertson Quay that they shared, they saw themselves through the excruciating finality of their breakup.

For years he'd tolerated with some bemusement the fact that she liked indulging in bondage play. There was this one guy, a grizzled American who looked like a CIA operative, who paid her small amounts of money at a time for private sessions in which she would agree to be tied up with bondage rope—not the heavy hemp rope used in Japanese *shibari* practice, that would be much too complicated—and he would watch her pretend to struggle free (without ever freeing herself, of course) and masturbate. He got his kicks, apparently, from seeing women bound and gagged and looking helpless—a sick sexual fetish to some people, of course— but it was really sort of funny in a ridiculously twisted way.

"He gets a fucking kick out of jerking off when I'm tied up," she'd told her boyfriend, "so if he's going to pay me for that, why the hell not? The funny thing is he doesn't fuck me. It's an excuse for his perversion."

But that night, the suspicious boyfriend smelled a fish and kept asking for details of their meeting. She finally relented and told him. Yes, it wasn't about her just posing like a helpless whimpering wench anymore. She did that, of course, but this time she had finished off the session by giving the guy a blowjob.

She had made sure to swallow and not spit, gulping down all the sperm to hide the evidence. Maybe she had a guilty look on her face. Who knows?

If she was trying to test his resolve, it didn't work. "Look here," he'd yelled at her. "I don't want a girlfriend who's a hooker. If I'd wanted that, I would have gone out and paid for one."

Fellating the perverted Yank was the last straw. Which she thought somewhat weird. They'd both been swingers when they'd met, after all, and they had been to private parties at various friends' houses where they swapped partners with sheer disregard for anyone's moral censure. (Yes, this kind of thing happens to real people, and it actually thrives in seemingly boring places like Singapore.) But, he explained, there was a difference: They'd had an arrangement, and by agreeing to wrap her pink-lipsticked lips around that guy's turgid tool (not to mention actually swallowing his seed), she had violated it.

She wasn't supposed to do anything other than pretend to struggle, and she certainly wasn't expected to make physical contact with an actual penis. The stupid people who believed that Bill Clinton had "never had sex" with Monica Lewinsky were fooling themselves, thinking that the only kind of sex that could be defined as sex was that of a genitally penetrative nature.

Well, that guy had penetrated her mouth and shot down her throat. So what do you call *that*?!!

The irony of it all wasn't lost on her. At that point she wasn't really a prostitute, not in the socially accepted sense. She was just having fun, having only turned twenty-one, and the thought of easy money while she was still an undergraduate was too intoxicating to refuse. "The thing is," she now says, "I know the feeling that the real escorts have—it's always good to know a few rich guys who want to buy your shit." Being young and freshly scrubbed in a sensually enticing way, which is how she generally looks even with minimal makeup, is a huge asset—in essence, a back channel to a cash pipeline. "I don't actually super-need the money. I know I can get it if I'm super-desperate. My parents are not poor or anything, but I'm so fucking proud, you know. I want to get my own income. I would rather do this than go to church on Sundays and depend on my parents. Why pretend that I am the daughter I am not, just for their money?"

That was how the whole deal went down. She was doing it less for the money and more for the kicks. It empowered her. A sexy woman, she says, is one who can express her sexuality any which way she chooses to, regardless of what she does for a living. Fashion models, rock stars, porn stars, who gives a toss what you are as long as you put your own personal stamp on things? Living any other way would be slavery, a form of indentured servitude to a set of social norms someone else designed. In her case, having these guys pay her to avail themselves of her sexual self, regardless of how that was actually expressed, counted as part and parcel of her chosen path in life.

"The whole thing started when I started modeling, and doing the whole fetish and nude thing, back when I was eighteen. I decided I wanted to model but I needed a photographer. The basic idea was that because I'm a girl most guys would just fucking die to snap a camera at, I knew that I didn't ever have to pay for my photo shoots as long as I was willing to take off my clothes—that's generally the rule with these amateur photographers—and so I was initially doing this just for the hell of it. I had a few guys agree to pay me to shoot me in glamour poses, often partially nude and sometimes fully naked.

"I doubled my going rate for the guys who wanted me in *Penthouse* or *Hustler* magazine poses and the funny thing is each time that happened, they didn't refuse and paid up. That's how badly they wanted to see me that way. So I posed and spread my legs. Showed them my pussy, did the two-finger salute, spread open my lips. Men are such basic animals and, I have to say, I loved knowing I could control their lust that way. I was actually the one in charge when they thought they were."

After she turned eighteen, she did less modeling and more freelance escorting. She had only three clients, including the American bondage guy, and never wanted to move beyond that.

"Any more than those three guys, it would feel like I was being a real professional and I didn't want that," she clarifies. "I wanted to be like a part-time prostitute, a student who could get straight As in her classes but did this pay-to-play thing on the side."

The only catch was, she found herself discovering, she felt a wee bit guilty about the manipulation involved. It was her secret life, to be sure, but it came with conditions. "I made it clear to all of them that the only way they could have me in any way other than platonic would be to pay me—I was very clear with them on that," she explains. "There's this other American guy, I know one time he told me to meet him and let's just have a great holiday and have no expectations about being paid. Which we did. We took a holiday together to New Zealand, and it was fine. He just gives me money because he wants to, not because I demand it. But you know, sometimes I think I should just join an escort agency and forget all this. I don't feel it's healthy for him. Because he really likes me and he knows this is the only way I will ever sleep with him. But now I think I am kind of embarrassed by the manipulation involved.

"I feel embarrassed about going out and pretending to be their girlfriend and for that they have to pay me. I know there will never be a real relationship, because I'm not in love with them. It's not about being embarrassed about transgressing a societal norm, it's not about that at all. It's about the instant when I take the money from them—I always feel sorry that I made them do that, because I really did enjoy my time with them. So there's something about it that's not real. When I am with them, I'm not really pretending that I really like them. On the other hand I know they are not the top priority in my life, which is what most sexual relationships should be, conventionally. But in this case it is not. There is an artificiality about it. It's like a stolen moment, sharing that with someone. Whereas outside that moment, I don't really like him. You know what I mean?"

She pauses for a bit. "It's not as if I see myself like a hypocrite. I know what I'm doing. I know why I'm doing it. You want something I'm not willing to give unless you pay me. Usually, it's not about doing it for a certain fee either. Usually, it's about 'What is my situation?' And if I need more money, they will give me more money. It's almost like I'm being 'kept' but by three different guys, to whom I relate in pretty much no other way than sexually. I never ever feel conflicted about that part, I never ever feel like I am just a prostitute selling my body.

"The only conflict I have is that I feel sorry that I make these guys pay for it. Because they're really nice guys and shouldn't have to. But I need the money. And it's not that I feel sorry for them—I like them all as people, but I'm not going to sleep with them unless they pay me—I make it very clear to them that the only way they can have me is to pay me, on the condition that I won't do anything I don't want to do."

It sounded easy enough, at first. Now she finds that the sheer depth of her conflict over her manipulation of men is naturally entwined with her personal boundaries, with all the things she's yearned to explore.

Waitress, one rope bondage, please, but keep the blowjob on the side?

Her obsession with selling herself this way then becomes so hard to explain. And this is why she's "Alexandra Leaving," the lost girl. And a girl at a loss for words.

Describing what she wants is not tough at all, it's just that not everybody gets it. "The guys are always less kinky than I am," she admits. "I like all sorts of shit. Back when I started out modeling and then doing this, just after I turned eighteen, I was into reenacting rape fantasies and having guys peeing on me. I never actually got raped, but the peeing, yes, I've done that. When I'm sufficiently drunk and especially if I am sort of in love with the guy, I want him to pee on me. Oh my God! It's fucking great."

That's the kind of thing usually only seen in Japanese porn movies. What on earth propels her to enjoy that kind of turn-on, the need to feel herself being urinated on by a man?

"I just like feeling fucking dirty!" she exclaims. "I've only done that in a real relationship, not for money, only for boyfriends. Normally we do it in the bathroom, and I'm jerking off while he pees on me. One time, I was having my period and I was masturbating in the shower, and I was peeing and he was peeing, and it was a whole fucking mess."

Her menstrual blood and his yellow fluid, what a wild way to mix it up! "The shower was on the whole time, though, so it wasn't too bad," she recalls. "But sometimes I don't know, I don't know if I'm just being immature. When it came to that American bondage guy, there were times when I stopped myself to ask whether I really liked him or if I was just doing bondage for his money. The truth is that I really like him as a person and actually if he didn't pay me any money, I might actually like him more. So in a way I sort of didn't like myself for it. It was one of those things that really grated on my nerves. Maybe I wanted to recapture that same feeling of being just eighteen and having a guy I was really crazy about express his love by peeing on me, when it was purely for the dirty, dirty pleasure of it rather than taking money for the thrill of it."

Then she tells a story about the one man she's never forgotten. She met him in Malaysia while on a short vacation there. "I met him in Kuala Lumpur. He's an American, fifty years old, a businessman, a real-estate guy. He just picked me up, super-casual, at the airport. At K.L. airport, of all places! He picked me up and we exchanged a few emails. I don't know why he really liked me. He just did. I was dressed in crappy clothes and shit. So, anyway, he wanted to take me on holiday and I thought, well, I can actually make money from this moonlighting thing so why not? What did I have to lose? So, I thought, okay, I'll go meet him. He went for STD tests and stuff 'cos he was paranoid, and I went for a blood test and a general STD test. Then we met up.

"I said to him, 'Give me S$500!' Not saying if I meant U.S. or Singapore dollars. And he immediately paid me in U.S. dollars! That was cool—this was back when the U.S. dollar exchange rate was like 1.8, you know, so it was great. We'd stay at his hotel suite in Singapore and go for dinner. He was nice to me and I liked him. There are some people you talk to and you feel like you're banging your head against a wall. I had only been with one other guy before this, in this sort of arranged way, and that guy, back when I first met him, it was a bit hard. But this guy, he was just very cool, I could just open up. It was all really simple to understand. He flew me to a lot of places. We moved around mostly in Asia, because he had a lot of business in Vietnam and Thailand. And he's got some places on the West Coast, in the U.S., so he took me to San Francisco."

They eventually fell out over a trip that was being planned, which she says she stupidly canceled. "We were supposed to go on this boat trip and then to Las Vegas and all that, but I got this call from a friend of mine who got a directing job in Australia and needed a model for a commercial. He said, 'Why don't you come to Sydney for the shoot?' and, well, I really liked this guy so I went. But now in retrospect I think: Shit, that American dude, he really fucking planned that fucking boat trip and the Vegas trip. He really planned it. And I screwed him over!

"I don't know what I was doing. In retrospect I was not very nice. I just said to him, 'I've got a job modeling in Sydney, and I can't come.' And he was just, well, like, 'Damn, I'm bummed.' I actually met him again recently while I was dating my last boyfriend, by sheer accident, and he looked really sad." They'd known one another for a whole year and had traveled together several times, so it was a weird way to end it. "I was traveling twice a month with him, and he was great in bed—he had an eight-inch dick and it was so fucking hard! Really, he was *so* great. Any escort would call him a dream client. He would just give me money, just according to what I needed because he knew my situation, he knew I was still a student so he paid me according to how much he thought I needed. The average was US$500."

There were only two such guys before him: the bondage guy and another man, an Englishman named Steve. "He was from London and was in Singapore on business. I only saw him one time and never again. We met online and had read each other's blogs and I guess there was some fascination and intrigue from that. I wasn't actively seeking to be paid for anything sexual. He emailed me and said, 'Do you want to come down to my place for the weekend? I'll give you some money.' And I thought, well, I'm eighteen, so what the fuck? Why the hell not? So I did. But I was kind of nervous because I wasn't with an agency or anything and I had only known this guy from reading his blog for a month, you know. Anyway, we stayed in the suite and made out and had sex. He gave me S$800, not much but a step-up from my first 'client,' the bondage guy, who paid me S$400 each time for two hours.

"The bondage guy, I was with him for months, and honestly it was a lot of fun. You have to remember, I was eighteen at the time, and it was my introduction to fine wine, cigars, and expensive food. That was the fucking kick for me. And the funny thing is now that I've grown up a bit, I feel a bit weird, like I resent it in a way. I do ask why I had to do it for the money when, really, I would have done it for free."

Ah, but therein lies the catch. Because he was willing to pay for the pleasure of her company, there was no way she was going to permit herself to do it for free. Her enraged boyfriend was right. Indisputably, by any definition of the word, she had willingly become a hooker.

Well, as the old saying goes, no rest for the wicked. In November 2007, she took the plunge and went to an escort agency to offer her services. She decided that turning pro was the only way out. That way she could ditch the bondage guy once and for all. He was her only regular pay-to-play pal and had indirectly caused the breakup of her real-life relationship. She could also create a metaphysical barrier. No one from her past would ever trespass. "Since I like older men who have money," she quipped, "It was a good way to get a date."

"I did my first trick with another girl, she called herself Maya, a really hot Malay girl. We went to the hotel and I thought we were going to be paid to do a threesome but it didn't turn out that way at all. When we got to the room, there were two guys waiting. One of them took Maya and the other took me, and we went to separate rooms. Wow, he was the sweetest guy on earth! I never liked a Chinese guy so much! And I never, never date Asian men, so this was totally out of the blue.

"What was really weird was the way he reminded me of my father—middle-aged, in his fifties, same build, also a an architect, also from Hong Kong! Maybe it's some kind of karmic payback for my childhood!"

The next day, the guy called her and took her out to the Orchard Road malls. They spent the day browsing and shopping, like a regular couple. There was no sex at all this time, which surprised yet didn't disappoint her. The guy genuinely liked her as a person.

She started thinking she could fall in love with him. She couldn't believe what was happening.

"And that," she now says, "was my own wishful thinking." He never called her again. She'd failed to get his phone number, assuming the agency would send for her again the next time he was in Singapore, but they never heard from him either.

She should have asked for his phone number! By not doing so, perhaps she'd led him to believe she wasn't interested. "Maybe he got cold feet and thought he'd better call it quits and disappear before we fall in love or something, who knows? You meet a real nice guy and he turns out to be a dickhead, just like the rest of them."

She stopped working for the agency. One pro-escort gig was enough to put her off for life.

It's bad enough having this secret life when you're still a student at Singapore Management University, but having your emotions played with—that's just too much to handle. She'd started with the bondage guy back when she was still in junior college! "My life is full of weird shit," she now concludes. "After I turned seventeen, I kept getting weirder and weirder. Now I don't know what to do with myself anymore."

Maybe it was time to stop and take stock of things, and to purge her wrecked emotions. She has started writing a novel, much of it based on herself. "My novel is about this girl called Alexandra and a forty-year-old man. He's this weirdo, really repressed, and it's kind of like a Lolita story except she's a little bit older. The girl's like crazy and wacky but she's a virgin and she wants to lose it. And this older guy, she's enchanted by him, and she follows him to Thailand where he's a sculptor. And there, he tells her: 'I can't fuck you, because you're so bloody young and I might get into trouble.'

"But that's the reason he gives himself. The bigger reason is that he just can't deal with it. He can't deal with women having their own minds. And she ends up confused because she wants him but only on her terms."

She pauses, stares into space, knits her brow, and frowns.

"I'm still trying," she says, "to work out the ending."

Postscript

Whoredom came naturally to them. To regard men
as cocks, differing only in shape and size and proficiency.
They could manipulate and create the most excruciating
embarrassments for their would-be lovers simply because
beyond being cocks and sources of money, men as individuals
did not interest them.

—James Eckardt, *Singapore Girl*

"Why do men pay for sex?" asks Giacomo Franchetti, an Italian expatriate who has been based in Singapore for the past eight years. "I know that I couldn't do it, not because I'm married but because I would see it as something below my dignity. It's for men who can't find women on their own, who have no choice but to pay to get female companionship. Maybe I am saying this because I am Italian, but I think you should always be able to find a woman on your own, whether that means dating someone or picking up a girl at a bar. I think paying for sex is something only men who are desperate do, men who are losers."

In the early months of 2008, several sex scandals grabbed the world news headlines, featuring men who might well qualify as losers in Giacomo's book. But were they really?

There was the strange case of Finnish Foreign Minister Ilkka Kanerva, fired from his job after word got out that he had sent no less than 200 text messages from his cellphone to a fetching blonde stripper named Johanna Tukiainen. He was sixty years old, she was twenty-nine. Most of the messages were of a blatantly sexual nature ("Do you want to do it in some exciting place? What could it be?" as reported by the wire service Agence France-Presse). Kanerva was a career politician, a Finnish Member of Parliament for thirty-three years who had held four posts in the cabinet and had been the country's Foreign Minister for the past year, a man tipped by some to be his country's future president. Whether he did or did not rendezvous with Ms Tukiainen in "some exciting place" remains unclear, but the damage had been done. The father of two daughters was unavailable for comment, having immediately gone "on sick leave" after admitting to the messages.

Kanerva's unraveling occurred the same week, coincidentally, as that of Max Mosley, the president of the International Automobile Federation (FIA) and one of the key players in the lucrative Formula One motor racing subculture followed by millions of fans. According to the British tabloid News of the World, Mosley had "enacted Nazi death camp scenes with five prostitutes," role-playing scenarios in which he gave orders in German while whipping the girls who were wearing "mock death-camp uniforms," all done in the course of a five-hour session in a London flat on March 28, 2008. (Curiously, Mosley admitted to doing this but denied anything smacking of Nazism. He explained that some of the girls only spoke German, hence his use of the language during the session!) Mosley, sixty-seven, also happens to be the son of Sir Oswald Mosley, the British parliamentarian who famously befriended Adolf Hitler (and even had Hitler attend his wedding as the guest of honor). Naturally, all this was of great interest to many Jewish racing drivers and motoring enthusiasts, who called for his dismissal.

And then, of course, there was Eliot Spitzer, the disgraced Governor of New York and previous two-time Attorney-General, who was investigated for using the services of an exclusive call-girl service called the Emperors Club VIP, which since December 2004 had catered to an upper-crust clientele willing to fork out for its "diamond girls" (which was how the girls were rated on its website—a "three-diamond" call girl meant US\$1,000 an hour, and there was also an elite Icon Club, with hourly fees starting at US\$5,500). Spitzer had, it turned out, been a major client of this escort agency (while he had been publicly working in his gubernatorial capacity as "Mr Clean" who favored busting prostitution rings in New York) and he had also resorted to illegal means to do so—he'd set up a fake company called QAT Consulting which hid his wire transfers to the Emperors Club as "business transactions."

Spitzer had been in the governor's chair for sixteen months when the chips came crashing down. The truly bizarre thing that came out of his decline and fall was the way in which he made his most famous courtesan-of-choice a media star. Spitzer was caught arranging to meet a girl in a hotel in Washington, D.C., on the night before Valentine's Day 2008. He had arranged for her to travel by train from New York's Penn Station to the hotel (itself a contravention of the Mann Act, which makes illegal any endeavour whereby a prostitute is transported across U.S. state lines) and paid her US$4,300 in cash with a bonus included as a security deposit of sorts for more future meetings.

The girl he wanted, "a petite, pretty brunette, five feet five inches tall and weighing 105 pounds" named "Kristen" was also outed in the bust, and revealed to be Ashley Alexandra Dupré, twenty-two, from New Jersey, according to a *New York Times* report.

Lovely Ashley then found her face splashed all over the newspapers, going from total anonymity to instant notoriety after she became the fifth-most-searched subject on *Google* that week. People started logging onto her *MySpace* and *Facebook* pages (she reportedly began to quickly delete her "connections" to her "friends" on *Facebook* as a result, even as her *MySpace* page racked up seven million new visits). She even became an Internet sensation when people started downloading her songs—she was an aspiring singer, and a single she had released called "What

We Want" suddenly found itself being played some three million times on the Internet, and another song "Move Ya Body" set the record for being the fastest to command top price on a music download site—all this reported by no less reliable an authority than *Bloomberg News*. She'd apparently moved to New York in 2004 to escape her background (broken home, drugs, abuse, and was finally broke and homeless), clearly resorting to escorting to pay the bills while waiting to be a star in the music world.

The enormity of the public fascination with her was undoubtedly appalling to the federal prosecutors, particularly since they were still hoping to gain her assistance (as a witness against Spitzer in the inevitable courtroom trial), but the fact remained that she had unwittingly served as a touchstone for many people who, as in the case with all celebrities, used her as a scrim for their own projections and feelings about the place of sex workers in general.

Presumably, some investigated her music out of sympathy, and surely others did so to satiate their cynicism (to hear for themselves if she could actually sing, of course), but what nobody seemed to notice was the exact historical lineage this connoted. Ashley Dupré was merely the modern-day version of the historically exalted courtesan, an iconic figure of beauty and charm, and what could even be less prosaic than the fact that she was a singer as well? In the days of the ancient Greeks, women were almost always kept at home to tend to either cooking or children, and the only Greek women allowed to walk unaccompanied in public were actresses, musicians, and courtesans.

Whatever the era, the services of a courtesan always come at a price, paid as a measure of faith, hope, and worship (as opposed to charity, since nobody ever works in the escort business out of charity). What did Ashley have that was so special, many people wondered, that would make a closet rake like Eliot Spitzer fork out US$4,300? (The willingness to forsake the use of condoms was one such specialty, Ashley later admitted, but she wasn't saying much more. Not, presumably, until the book and movie deal were closed.) There are apparently things that make an escort worth her price, while her lowly streetwalker sisters ply their trade for much, much less.

Not everyone is that fussy, though, and the sex tourist is often spoiled for choice, especially in Asia. In Singapore, for instance, the Thai, Cambodian, Laotian, and Vietnamese ladies of the night, on any given night, will settle for S$250 while the Filipinas working the Duxton Hill bars have been known to charge as much as S$500.

Only the upscale escorts at the other end of the food chain will meet their clients much more discreetly, usually in some swanky hotel's top-tier suite, for S$1,600 a night. Short-time, quickie deals are often struck at S$800 (S$500 for the girl, S$300 for the agency) so the overnight deal is often better for all concerned (S$1,000 for the girl, S$600 for the agency). Some girls have been known to complain, but never about the money—usually, it's about the nature of the job or the client.

Shakira, one night in late 2007, talks of weighing the pros and cons of getting her thousand bucks while having to endure the all-night snoring of a corpulent, beached whale. "At least he's nice," she concedes, "and he's already promised to take me to Las Vegas to celebrate the new year. When I got to the hotel, he immediately had us upgraded to the Presidential Suite. I think he's got some serious connections with the hotel management. I can't say the sex was great, though. Fat men just can't do it right. Plus he's not circumcized. I hate all that foreskin when I'm giving a blowjob!"

There are other occupational hazards unique to her profession. The interminable waiting around in hotel lobbies when the clients don't show up. The constant need to check her cellphone, often placed on silent mode whenever she's out in public with her "normal" friends. The obsessive-compulsive behavior that comes with leading a secretive double life.

Openness to sex (or, more specifically, the idea of having sex with strangers) is a job prerequisite, somewhat like secretaries being hired because they can type. The ads for escort work in the classifieds sections of the newspapers always ask for "open-minded" candidates—a curious euphemism since the old joke is that they're not hired because their minds are open but rather because their thighs are. The girls sustain such open-mindedness by, ironically, closing their minds to doubt and disbelief—like fears of being caught out by a platonic friend or nosy neighbor, and sublimated anxieties pertaining to supposedly ill-gotten gains; several girls have confessed discomfort with the idea of "dirty money." (One Singaporean girl, after being paid by her client, would ask a friend to exchange the bills with "clean money" before giving the cash to her ailing grandmother.)

Others admit to monthly periods of stress when it's time to head down to the clinic for the standard STD tests. Words suddenly take on new meaning—words like chlamydia, gonorrhea, syphilis, herpes, and hepatitis—as they dress down in tee shirts and jeans before trooping down to places like the Singapore DSC Clinic at 31 Kelantan Lane, off Jalan Besar, for a blood test which yields results after a harrowing three-hour wait. Kelantan Lane is the preferred choice of many escorts and other sex workers, since it assures anonymity, which only serves to highlight the undercover nature of the girls' double lives.

Some psychologists have referred to what they do as a form of "delusional psychosis" (the term also being applied to serial killers and others operating on their own uncontrollable urges), but much of this secrecy and subterfuge is founded on metaphysical leanings. Money is, from the outset, always the driving force but it takes a specific mindset to continually work this way.

What they really sell is a sense of illusory intoxication—by intoxicating men with the stereotypical image of a sensually aware, sexually submissive Asian girl. That, entwined with the need to evoke pleasure in its often disguised forms, along with the sense of the taboo that gives it value. For example, in *Diary of a Thai Escort*, published in 2008 by Heaven Lake Press in Bangkok and written by "Anonymous" (since the girl in question refused to use even a pseudonym), a naive young Thai sex worker reveals her experiences of living and working in London, astounded at first that she could get £150 for a quickie (with £50 going to her pimp) and do outcall work starting at £210 an hour (with £70 going to the pimp).

She also discloses how many of them end up in the U.K., paying anything from £6,000 to £9,000 to secure a visa and plane ticket, finally paying off the debts and making back the money literally on their backs. It's a form of indentured servitude, even though some free themselves of the burden after three months by making what regular bargirls back home would make if they worked themselves silly for a whole year.

On their days off, her fellow Thai sisters get together over meals of home-cooked *pad thai* noodles and discuss their week's adventures, their accomplishments at bilking their *farang* blokes. "Candy was telling us about the faces she makes when she wants to make a customer feel sexy," she recalls. "She says that she makes a sexy face and then takes off her bra slowly and that makes a customer so horny that they come really quickly. I practised in front of the mirror and she showed me how to get my mouth just right. I kept laughing but it worked."

She thinks it funny, yet many cannot resist the clarion call of the sexy siren. "The prospect of a new sexual partner is one of the things I enjoy most about paid sex, brothels, and sex in general," says Jeffrey Kaminsky, who'd flown from his home in Los Angeles, California, to savor the fleshy delights of Thailand and Singapore. "The new partner and how they will perform is what lures me, as I'm sure it does most men, to brothels to sample the new recruits. Nothing really gets my heart pounding like the anticipation of being with a new girl, as I watch her walking ahead of me, hips swaying, and I fantasize about what she will look like without her clothes, what she will do, what tricks she knows."

"And sex with a professional is always better than with an amateur, except maybe in Singapore," he laughs. "I have to say, though, that the number of times I've had great-to-amazing sex far outweighs the times I've been disappointed." Kaminsky says he still indulges in his personal fantasy of "moving to Thailand and spending my days fucking Thai hotties in between incredible meals on the beach." He harbors no qualms about the transactional nature of such perfectly temporary liaisons, due in part to his own failed marriage and his cultural baggage as an American. "A date in the West is not a date but a comparison of resumes, backgrounds, estates, and financial portfolios with an eye towards a possible merger. Why shouldn't sex be a business transaction on a smaller scale?

"A lot of American women I know tell me the most important and awkward part of any relationship is when they are finally going to bed and what the guy will think of her if she agrees too soon. Worse, will the guy bail if she holds out too long? By agreeing to exchange one commodity for another, we cut to the chase. Personally, I have developed much more interesting and real relationships with girls who accept money for sex than with those who don't."

Interesting and real relationships? Most escorts harbor no such illusions.

"To me, these are not real men, they're customers," Shakira says. "I can't have sex with a real guy now, not the way I used to, because of this job. I think of all men the same way. I keep thinking I'm giving away for free what I charge S$1,000 a night for, and why should they get it for free? And some of the guys take photos of me with their cellphones, which I don't mind as long as they tip me extra. If I do it naked with my legs spread, I'll cover my face or put a pillow over my head. I know in the end they just want a souvenir to show, to brag to their guy friends. Look at her! Yes, I'm the girl they just fucked in the photo! And I don't mind that really, but the problem now is that I think I've identified myself too closely with how I make a living.

"When you do this kind of work, your mind really gets warped. Just the other day a bunch of us got together to eat on River Valley Road, at the famous Boon Tong Kee Chicken Rice, and you should've heard the way we were talking. 'Oh, you did that with him? Wow, that's so good, well done! You're really becoming a very good prostitute now! I'm so proud of you!' We were giggling and all that. I'm not kidding you. Can you imagine an ordinary group of girls getting together for a hen party and having that kind of conversation? We talk like this all the time."

She and her best friend Tiffany often compare new vibrators that their clients have bought them as gifts, when they're not comparing expensive handbags and shoes that came from the same source. Their colleague Maya went off with a famous Hollywood actor to an island off the coast of West Malaysia, and that was the hot topic for them that week at their little makeshift escort salon where they gather to gossip. They also talk about how the industry is changing, about girls escorting through the Internet. *Best Singapore Escorts* (found at *www.bestsingaporeescorts.com*) was one site, featuring actual photos of the girls and a rundown of their assets. Angel is twenty-three years old, 175 cm tall and weighs 53 kg, her figure is 92C-60-90 (measured in metric, of course) and she can be booked for either one, two, three, or six hours, or overnight. That kind of thing. But when one of Shakira's friends tried calling them from the phone number given on the site, nobody answered.

Other sites are more professional, and guys can book the girls to meet them at designated hotel rooms (no-shows are fined S$20), and they have an assortment of fees: "Promo prices" starting at

S$89.89 for a "new girl" or between S$140 to S$180 for a Thai girl with "two sessions within ninety minutes, inclusive of hotel room charges. Malaysian girls in Geylang start at S$150 for forty-five minutes, so this must appear a real bargain. The sites offer this exact same rate for girls from Korea, Colombia, and Russia, while "models" who have posed for adult magazines in Europe and the United States go for S$280. The downside is that many of these women are not subjected to mandatory health checks or STD tests, so the guys may never know what they're really getting.

Singaporean escorts like Maya, Shakira, and Tiffany will tell anyone who asks that staying with their upscale agency provides a much better lifestyle, where they don't have to worry as much about their health and get dinners, gifts, and overseas jaunts thrown in for good measure, as long as the pipeline keeps being built. The influx of casinos in Singapore, due in 2009, might well rejuvenate their business. The KTV bars have already thrown them a huge challenge, their armies of China girls already putting their stamp on the market—by reputation, they're known to be adept at pleasing their customers by any means necessary. "Things we would usually never do, like sex without condoms," says Tiffany, "although I myself have done that once because I couldn't turn down the offer."

The male mind is always mindful of how a girl, any girl, can do anything once, for the right price. Because a woman, unlike a man, can always be persuaded to change her mind. Whoever said the mating dance was over once money changes hands is dead wrong. It's just a different kind of dance. And these girls follow the beat of very different drummers.

The novelist Richard Mason, who wrote the 1957 classic *The World of Suzie Wong*, explained that the book was born when he checked into his hotel in Hong Kong and discovered that it was a popular pick-up spot for hookers. "I realized that it was virtually a brothel. I was thrilled. At that time, I had no idea at all, and thought it was just an ordinary hotel. But I thought, 'This is fabulous, I've found it!' From that moment, I knew I had my book. I thought that was unbelievable—like a gift from God."

The gift took shape in his story about the expatriated English artist Robert Lomax and his love affair with a Wan Chai prostitute, played by Nancy Kwan in the more famous 1960 movie (with William Holden as Lomax). There were also two theatrical versions (France Nuyen and Tsai Chin playing Suzie on Broadway in New York and the London West End respectively), and a cultural icon took hold.

Mason's beautiful Chinese bargirl was a human being, curiously dignified in her own willful way. "What's happened? This heat gone to your head?" she asks Lomax when he proposes marriage to her. "You're a big man. Maybe one day they will make you a lord. Mr Lord Lomax . . . Then I'd be Mrs Lord. Mrs Lord Bargirl. 'How do you do, Mrs Lord Bargirl? I hear you had 2,000 sailors before you were married.'"

That's the kind of spunk any dashing libertine might expect of an escort in the modern world, even as he also suspects that marriage to one might not result in a happy ending, at least not the fairy-tale kind. But the game endures, because the chase is programmed into the genetic code of men, lured by sirens with secrets.

And the sirens themselves must contend with their own lives as women, with what they themselves are worth.

Is an escort merely a glorified prostitute? What is her worth, then, as a human being?

Every night, there are young women who ask themselves these kinds of questions as they ascend the hotel elevators and head for the rooms. The night is young, they tell themselves. They have plenty of time to deal with the answers.

Acknowledgments

Several people were instrumental in making this book a reality, and I'd like to thank: Natalie Thompson, my editor, for her eagle eye, encouragement and enthusiasm; Alishia Yusman, my assistant, for accompanying me on some of the interviews and fact-checking certain essential details; Vivienne Yeo, friend and famous poet, for offering her comments and insights on some of the chapters; and, not least of all, my fellow scribes and kindred spirits—Meihan Boey, John Burdett, Isabella Chen, Mark Hillman, Barney Hoskyns, Brenda Scofield, Mika Tan, Paul Theroux, Bjorn Turmann and Jeff Wozniak—for their hours of conversation on the subject of escorts and the ethics of escorting.

If I've left anyone out, it's probably for your own personal safety and reputation.

Thanks also to Sheridan Prasso for our discussions following her own excellent book *The Asian Mystique: Dragon Ladies, Geisha Girls, and Our Fantasies of the Exotic Orient*, which I'd recommend without hestitation to anyone with even a remotely fetishistic interest in the subject of Asian exotica. I am also indebted to Jonathan Lobban and Christian Barker for their camaraderie when they were my editors at *August Man* magazine, for it was under their brave aegis that certain portions of this book were previously excerpted.

None of this would have been possible at all without the participation of all the interviewees quoted (and since all names were changed, only you know who you are). I would, however, like to apologize to two young women who initially agreed but then declined; one had cold feet and stood me up, the other was apparently getting married (and so both obviously decided that exposing the past might not be such a good idea after all!)—to both of you, I'd like to say that I had no intention of ever freaking you out and I sincerely wish you both well, now that you've both left the business.

A special word of appreciation, in this light, to Maya, who kept in touch with me despite changes of cellphone numbers, and who trusted in my discretion despite the details of her almost imaginary and very complicated life.

And, as always, to P.H., for her ongoing trust in me whenever I embarked on yet more field research in the name of armchair anthropology. I think we've redefined the term "high-fidelity" (as first defined by Nick Hornby).

Nina Hartley once told me that "the difference between erotica and pornography is lighting." I'd like to add, being devoid of cameras, that it's also hopefully in the writing.

Suggested Reading

These books provided the literary backdrop for my work over the past year, and I would like to recommend them for those seeking further reading:

Albert, Alexa: *Brothel: Mustang Ranch and Its Women*. New York: Random House, 2001.

Angell, Jeannette. *Callgirl: Confessions of an Ivy League Lady of Pleasure*. New York: HarperCollins, 2004.

Anonymous. *Diary of a Thai Escort*. Bangkok: Heaven Lake Press, 2008.

Brown, Louise. *Sex Slaves: The Trafficking of Women in Asia*. London: Virago Press, 2000.

Burdett, John. *Bangkok 8*. New York: Alfred A. Knopf, 2003.

Burdett, John. *Bangkok Tattoo*. London: Corgi Books, 2006.

Burdett, John. *Bangkok Haunts*. New York: Alfred A Knopf, 2007.

De Jour, Belle. *The Intimate Adventures of a London Call Girl*. London: Phoenix/Orion, 2005.

Delacoste, Frederique and Priscilla Alexander (editors.). *Sex Work: Writings by Women in the Sex Industry*. San Francisco: Cleis Press, 1987.

Eckardt, James. *Singapore Girl: A Memoir*. Singapore: Monsoon Books, 2006.

Elias, James E., Vern Bullough, Veronica Elias, and Gwen Brewer.(editors) *Prostitution: On Whores, Hustlers and Johns.* New York: Prometheus Books, 1998.

Field, Genevieve, and Rufus Griscom. (editors) *Nerve: Literary Smut.* New York, Broadway Books, 1998.

Fleiss. Heidi. *Pandering.* Los Angeles: Publisher's Group West, 2003.

Gaitskill, Mary. *Bad Behavior.* New York: Random House, 1988.

Griffin, Susan. *The Book of the Courtesans: A Catalogue of Their Virtues.* New York: Broadway Books, 2001.

Hickman, Katie. *Courtesans: Money, Sex and Fame in the Nineteenth Century.* New York: HarperCollins, 2003.

Holden, Kate. *In My Skin: A Memoir.* New York: Arcade, 2006.

Hollander, Xaviera, with Robin Moore and Yvonne Dunleavy. *The Happy Hooker: My Own Story (30th Anniversary Edition).* New York: ReganBooks, 2002.

Hollander, Xaviera. *Child No More: A Memoir.* New York: ReganBooks, 2002.

Kelman, Nick. *Girls.* New York, Back Bay Books, 2004.

Lewis, Sarah Katherine. *Indecent: How I Make It and Fake It as a Girl for Hire.* Emeryville, California: Seal Press, 2006.

Mason, Richard. *The World of Suzie Wong.* New York: HarperCollins, 1982.

Moore, Christopher G. *A Killing Smile.* Bangkok: Heaven Lake Press, 2004.

Nostitz, Nick. *Patpong: Bangkok's Twilight Zone.* London: Westzone Publishing, 2000.

Odzer, Cleo. *Patpong Sisters: An American Woman's View of the Bangkok Sex World*. New York: Blue Moon Books, 1994.

Olsen, Warren. *Confessions of a Bangkok Private Eye*. Singapore: Monsoon Books, 2006.

Pan, L.Q. and Richard Lord (editors) *Best of Singapore Erotica*. Singapore: Monsoon Books, 2006.

Pisani, Elizabeth. *The Wisdom of Whores: Bureaucrats, Brothels and the Business of AIDS*. London: Granta, 2008.

Prasso, Sheridan. *The Asian Mystique: Dragon Ladies, Geisha Girls and Our Fantasies of the Exotic Orient*. New York: PublicAffairs/Perseus, 2005

Sheehan, Jack. *Skin City: Behind the Scenes of the Las Vegas Sex Industry*. New York: HarperCollins, 2006.

Tasso. Valerie. *Insatiable: The Sexual Adventures of a French Girl in Spain*. London: Corgi Books. 2005.

Tisdale, Sallie. *Talk Dirty to Me: An Intimate Philosophy of Sex*. New York: Doubleday, 1994.

Queen, Carol. *Real Live Nude Girl: Chronicles of Sex-Positive Culture*. San Francisco: Cleis Press, 1997.

Warren, James Francis. *Ah Ku and Karayuki-San: Prostitution in Singapore, 1870-1940*. Singapore: Singapore University Press, 2003.

Weitzer, Ronald. (editor) *Sex for Sale: Prostitution, Pornography and the Sex Industry*. New York: Routledge, 2000.

Whitehead, Kate and Nury Vittachi. *After Suzie: Sex in South China*. Hong Kong: Chameleon Books, 1997.

If you like this you'll like ...

If you enjoyed *Invisible Trade II*, Monsoon Books has other titles by Gerrie Lim, which you'll be sure to want to read.

INVISIBLE TRADE

High-class sex for sale in Singapore

Gerrie Lim

When an ambitious, adventurous gent named Sir Thomas Stamford Raffles "discovered" the tiny Southeast Asian island of Singapore in 1819, claiming it for the British Crown, he envisioned it as a geographical gateway between East and West. Now an independent city-state, Singapore is considered an Asian economic miracle, still a strategic crossroads, but its position on the map has also garnered bluechip status in the international sex industry. Thanks to the constant influx of business travelers, a floating world exists that few talk about, where beautiful escorts from various countries offer discreet companionship for a price, one not usually proffered in the bars and brothels of Asia.

Writer Gerrie Lim investigated this phenomenon and gained access to the secret world of highpriced sex workers. The result is a series of lucid portraits offering insights into this remarkable area of modern commerce. His subjects are women who are lavishly rewarded with money and gifts, some diverging from the oft-trod path to perform kinky services that include whipping and spanking, others being flown to exotic resorts in the company of men with money to burn. He also enters the shadowy domain of gay male escorts and karaoke hostesses, whose views challenge societal norms and question assumptions made about their career choices. The result is a fascinating work of cultural observation, from the vantage point of an eloquent literary voice.

ISBN: 978-981-05-1033-6

(Monsoon Books, 2004)

IN LUST WE TRUST

Adventures in Adult Cinema

Gerrie Lim

Intrepid journalist and bestselling author Gerrie Lim invites you to join him on an unusual road trip, through his adoptive home town of Los Angeles, California, and its deceptively suburban San Fernando Valley—the ground-zero of the ever-booming, US$12-billion American porn industry.

His chronicle spans a ten-year cycle, during which he interviewed adult-film superstars like Jenna Jameson, Jill Kelly and Silvia Saint, shared with Asia Carrera and Annabel Chong mutual thoughts on being Asian in a largely non-Asian field, and filed reportage from film shoots as the "Cinema Blue" columnist for *Penthouse Variations* as well as stories about adult Internet technologies as the International Correspondent for *AVN Online*.

In the trailblazing vein of his previous book *Invisible Trade* (about the escorting industry), this compelling new work combines sizzling elements of sex and celebrity to document a curious and complex world. Enter, then, the perverse universe of the porn star, laced with Lim's candidly offbeat observations and dangerously wry wit.

ISBN: 978-981-05-5302-9

(Monsoon Books, 2006)